THE PRESENTATION
OF REALITY

T0370621

THE PRESENTATION
OF REALITY

BY

HELEN WODEHOUSE, D.Phil.

Author of *The Logic of Will*; Lecturer in Philosophy
in the University of Birmingham

Cambridge:
at the University Press
1910

CAMBRIDGE
UNIVERSITY PRESS

University Printing House, Cambridge CB2 8BS, United Kingdom

Cambridge University Press is part of the University of Cambridge.

It furthers the University's mission by disseminating knowledge in the pursuit of
education, learning and research at the highest international levels of excellence.

www.cambridge.org
Information on this title: www.cambridge.org/9781107426177

© Cambridge University Press 1910

This publication is in copyright. Subject to statutory exception
and to the provisions of relevant collective licensing agreements,
no reproduction of any part may take place without the written
permission of Cambridge University Press.

First published 1910
First paperback edition 2014

A catalogue record for this publication is available from the British Library

ISBN 978-1-107-42617-7 Paperback

Cambridge University Press has no responsibility for the persistence or accuracy of
URLs for external or third-party internet websites referred to in this publication,
and does not guarantee that any content on such websites is, or will remain, accurate
or appropriate.

NOTE

SCATTERED passages in this Essay have appeared in an article called "Knowledge as Presentation," in *Mind* for July, 1909. The appendix to Chapter VII, "Professor James on Conception," was published in *The Journal of Philosophy, Psychology, and Scientific Method* in September, 1909. My thanks are due to the editors of these Journals for permission to republish.

H. W.

August, 1910.

CONTENTS

INTRODUCTION

THE theory of knowledge may be fairly considered, from one point of view, as a psychological preface to metaphysics. It is common to urge that there are great difficulties and dangers in the method of approaching the latter through psychology instead of through logic, and it is true enough that such difficulties exist, yet their existence seems hardly to excuse us from endeavouring to open both roads. Complete philosophy after all is bound to the task of connecting and reconciling all our beliefs. It should therefore have nothing to fear from a sound psychology, and psychology itself has much to gain by becoming and remaining, in some part at least, philosophical.

The following essay is therefore intended for a description of knowledge from the point of view of a philosophical psychology. The first part, and the longest, will deal with knowledge in the narrower sense, where we have true judgments about the actual world; the second part (a very short one) will deal with Error, the third with Imagination. I desire to maintain and to illustrate the doctrine that in all cognitive experience we come into immediate contact with objective reality, of the existence of which we have in experience an irrefutable witness; and that on all levels of cognition, sensuous or intellectual, this happens in the same way, namely, by the presentation of an object to a subject[1]. I write on psychology in order to make from it a preface to metaphysics, and desire to keep as clear as I can from writing on metaphysics itself. That is, I shall try to describe the process of knowing reality, but shall always endeavour to put aside if possible the question of the nature and origin of reality.

Whatever his opinions, a student of the theory of knowledge can have but one sentiment at present towards those who are leading the work in this field. I should wish this essay to express some of the gratitude and admiration which all of us must feel for the work of so brilliant a group of scholars from all nations. My personal gratitude is due in two directions in particular:—firstly to the extraordinarily suggestive works of Professor Alexius Meinong; secondly, and from first to last, to everything that English-speaking students connect with the honoured name of Dr G. F. Stout.

[1] With regard to this matter, as to all the rest of psychology, I am indebted for more than I can ever state to the teaching of Dr James Ward.

PART I

KNOWLEDGE

CHAPTER I

KNOWLEDGE AS PRESENTATION

SPEAKING generally, one may say that psychologists of all schools are agreed on the doctrine that cognition is an indispensable and fundamental element in mental life, which means, in non-technical language, that every conscious being in every instant of consciousness is partly engaged in knowing. So much we may take to be non-controversial, but the next step unfortunately takes us across the border in a moment. The present writer desires to take the side of those who maintain that in every instant of consciousness the conscious being knows *something*. We maintain, that is (to return to the technical form), that the fundamental relation of life involves the presentation of an object to a subject.

Expanding this doctrine, we maintain that even from the vaguest beginnings the process of consciousness has two sides. On the one hand it is reception—something comes to me. On the other hand I am active in reception, and I respond in feeling and striving to that which I receive. Naturally it is long before I learn to

1—2

describe my life in any such terms: nevertheless from the beginning I find something present with me, "something there"; and I try to get more of it or to get rid of it. At every moment I receive and respond, I desire and am answered or resisted, I seek and find.

What I find is the only thing that is capable of being found, namely the real world. My finding of it, my coming upon it and against it, is the event of the presentation of reality, and this is all that the phrase need mean. What meets us is the real, and this meeting, this having it before us in our conscious life, this finding it under our eyes, is presentation, or cognition, or knowledge. It has been said by an ingenious writer that to have a presentation cannot be to know an object, since the presentation itself is an additional reality requiring to be known[1]. With our sense of the term this objection does not hold, since "to have a presentation," for us, means simply to have something presented, to find something, to come up consciously against the real world—to know reality.

There would seem to be something curiously artificial in accounts of experience which leave out this aspect of direct meeting with something real. Professor James[2], in an early essay, describes cognition as a feeling which is taken to be in some way self-transcendent. We suppose, he says, that there must be a reality outside to resemble the feeling's quality, and we deny the function of knowledge to any feeling whose quality or content we do not believe to exist outside of that feeling as well as in it.

---

[1] H. A. Prichard, "The Psychologists' Treatment of Knowledge," in *Mind*, 1907, p. 50.

[2] "On the Function of Cognition" (*Mind*, O.S. x.).

Now the feeling itself cannot discover whether or not such a reality exists. Its own quality is the only quality it grasps, and its own nature is not a particle altered by having the self-transcendent function of cognition either added to it or taken away. The function is "accidental"; it falls outside and not inside its being.

It is scarcely fair to criticise this passage at present because its form of statement has so evidently been determined by remembrance of the existence of error, and of that we shall have later on to give our own account. But we are justified even here in observing how artificial the description appears at first sight to be. Had it not been for the consideration of error, it is likely that no one would ever have thought of separating an event of knowing from what is known, or of saying that to see a thing is an accidental function of seeing[1]. Professor James's expressions would have been thought to be at least dangerous and misleading. Our own account has at least the merit of simplicity—that knowledge is that side of experience on which we meet with reality.

One-sided and Double-sided Terms.

Since every mental process in the concrete has the two sides of action and reception, of the subject putting itself forth and the object coming in upon it, it is natural that psychology should bestow its names sometimes upon

---

[1] Cf. Mr A. Hoernlé, "Image, Idea, and Meaning," in *Mind*, 1907; "'To mean something' is after all a conscious act, and the self-transcension of consciousness inherent in all objective reference is something experienced by us. The fundamental fact...is that in experience we are conscious of reality."

the sides taken separately and sometimes upon the two taken as a whole. It follows that some common terms refer only to the subject side or only to the object side of consciousness, whilst other terms, or the same terms in other contexts, stand for concrete processes including both aspects, and from this fact some confusion may occasionally arise. "Feeling" for instance in the technical psychological sense is subjective only, whilst "emotion" usually includes some presentation as well[1]. "Discovery" applies both to the object found and to the activity of finding it. "Decision" may stand for the act of deciding or for the thing decided on or for both together. "Assumption" covers both the deliberate creation of an object and the presentation of it as it is created; as well as standing for the created object itself. "Knowledge" is sometimes abstract or "one-sided," but is often a double-sided term, and in that case the names of the two aspects it includes are "presentation" and its correlative "apprehension."

The two Sides of Knowledge.

Let us for our present purpose take "knowledge" to be concrete, containing in itself the two aspects of consciousness, and let us attend for a moment to each of them in turn.

1. "The content of knowledge" as opposed to "knowing," we may fairly use to represent one side of the process. Knowledge in this sense belongs to the side of the object, and consists in the presentation of reality in consciousness.

[1] The popular use of these two terms is usually just the reverse of this.

A certain reluctance to allow these contents of knowledge to fall to the object side comes sometimes from a confusion of the psychological with the physiological use of "subjective." The physiologist is naturally apt to class as subjective everything that is "in the mind," and certainly whatever is known must be presented in the mind. It will be sufficient for our purpose if we point out that this classification would be useless to the psychologist; for his region of interest begins only after the threshold of consciousness has been passed, and therefore his distinction of subjective and objective must fall not between mind and body but within "the mind" itself. The world comes to me in the fields of sensation and thought as an object known, and I in feeling and striving react upon it. This reaction is subjective, but the contents of knowledge are objective for the psychologist, for they constitute the shape in which the object comes to me.

2. The subjective element in knowing is apprehension, the word being used in its ordinary meaning as the correlative of presentation, and not in its etymological sense. It is activity, but of a special and peculiar kind, being the activity of reception only. In apprehending I do nothing to my object. I simply keep my eyes open and see.

We guard ourselves by this description against more than one mode of expression which seems to be dangerous. One such mode is found in the statement of many idealists that in knowledge we construct reality. This is a brief formulation of what for idealist metaphysics is of course a truth, but in the theory of knowledge it would seem to need expansion and qualification if it is not to be misinterpreted. Even if the whole world grows by means of our interest, of our questioning and seeking and demanding: even if nothing can exist except on condition that it is known : even then our knowing is not in any ordinary sense an act of construction or creation. Even in deliberate fiction or assumption, where we do wilfully create the objects that we apprehend, the creation is not the apprehension. Whatever our metaphysics may be it is most important to keep this psychological distinction clear. Whatever creates the reality that we find it is not the finding as such that creates it, and it is this finding that constitutes knowledge.

In the same way we must object to those forms of speech which seem to take certain events of knowing, judgment for instance, to be something more than the reception of presentation. It may be wise to distinguish judgment from some other kinds of apprehension, as occurring only after doubt has supervened, or as being concerned with a special kind or level of object, or with connections between objects, or what not. But if it is an element in knowing as such, then it must still be itself a kind of apprehension, a case of "finding something there." We must be suspicious, therefore, of descriptions of judgment which make it an "assertion," or an "assent," or a response to an imperative[1]; because these accounts seem likely to bring into judgment something more than pure knowledge. This would not matter, of course, except that we are so likely to slip back afterwards into thinking of the event so named as if it were still pure knowledge.

Still more must we object to those accounts which take

[1] E.g. Rickert, *Gegenstand der Erkenntniss*, 66, and Lipps, *Fühlen, Wollen, und Denken*, 187.

judgment (still not distinguished from knowing) to be a kind of appreciation or an acceptance or rejection. Our knowledge of an object may of course be a result of appreciation, in that we wanted to know; and appreciation must of course have cognition as a ground. But, if there is any meaning or use in distinguishing right from left or front from back or coming from going, then to know is not the same as to appreciate. The matter is confused by the fact that a propositional form of words may express much more than a judgment. "That won't do" covers the ordinary judgment "that doesn't fit," "that is unlike"; and the introspective judgment "that is not what I want"; and the imperative "take it away; let it go"; and the suggestion "let us look for something else." To compound all these meanings and to call the total a judgment, in the sense in which judgment is an element of knowledge, would seem to be a mere blurring of all the distinctions which it has taken psychology so long to make. One becomes suspicious of even so respectable a phrase as "knowledge in the concrete," because it turns out so often to mean something more concrete than knowledge. Cognition is no more an independent mental process than conation is; they are two elements in every possible mental process; and it is darkening of counsel to call them by each other's names.

Act and Object of Apprehension.

It is useless to deny that throughout this essay we shall be on controversial ground. From its very beginning our description of knowledge has committed us to distinguishing on every level of knowledge, even the lowest, between our act of apprehension or recipience and that which we receive. The acceptance or rejection of this distinction is so fundamental a point in any theory of consciousness that it is not easy to argue about it; I can only say that without such a distinction I do not see how to describe our experience of reality. If cognition is not the apprehension of an object, how can we know the world?

It may be that there is a reasonable answer to this question which I have been unable to find, and that the psychologists of a different school are in the right. I urge only that in any case they have no right to treat the question as irrelevant. If I have not misunderstood them, certain writers[1] tend to claim a curiously isolated position for their psychology, and an exemption from the duty of answering any question which may be supposed to be put to them by philosophers, even by common-sense philosophers. They hold fast to the doctrine that psychology is a natural science concerned with nothing but its own object of study; that this object of study consists in a series of conscious processes or states of consciousness, into which no distinction of subject and object need enter; and that it is not their business but the business of philosophy to get from such states to a person and a universe.

Now this would be very well if such writers would confine themselves to so purely scientific a position as that which is taken, for instance, by the geometry of non-Euclidean space. As I understand it, the student of such a geometry may be quite indifferent to the question

[1] Professor Titchener for instance? See his *Experimental Psychology of the Thought-Processes*.

whether such space is or is not in any way actually existent. That question is really left to the philosopher, and the philosopher is left with a free hand to answer it in the way he finds best. But the psychologists of whom I speak leave the philosopher no such freedom. They claim without any doubt to be writing of what is actual. We need not take the non-Euclidean parallels and found upon them our actual experience of space, but we have to take the self-contained streams of consciousness, with no relation of subject and object within them, and to transform them somehow into a society of real people living in a real world; knowing it, loving or hating it, and seeking their own ends within it.

If a science dictates to philosophy in this way, the philosopher must make a counter-claim to some supervision of the science; and his first request will naturally be that the object should be examined with which the science professes to start. The question will be whether these streams of self-contained feelings are actual at all, *and the burden of proof will be on those who assume them.* What is undoubtedly actual is the living being who knows things and seeks ends, even if they are no higher than the ends of a jelly-fish. Can a science, which claims to deal with the actual, venture to start with any description of its object which omits all reference to what is sought and what is known? My own opinion is that it must not; that, as the thinnest tablet must have two sides, so the most elementary consciousness must still be made up of recipience and response. This may be a mistaken opinion, but I insist that the burden of proof is not on its supporters but on their opponents. Unless reason is shown to the contrary, knowing cannot be taken as a self-contained feeling which somehow "claims" to be transcendent. Failing reason to the contrary, it must be taken in the ordinary and familiar way as *knowledge of something*.

Certain other writers, who have no difficulty in accepting this position so far as concerns intellectual cognition, find a difficulty when they come to sensation. In a sensation, they hold, no distinction can be made between subject and object, between sensing and sensatum, reception and what is received. All exists in an "immediate unity." This opinion is so well established that a special chapter must presently be devoted to it. I will only say here that just the same arguments seem to me to apply to sensation as apply on higher levels; and that therefore even sensation, elementary as it is, must on my view be still considered as knowledge of an object by a subject, and must involve on the one hand the sensing and on the other hand the sensatum. At present at any rate I shall assume that even on the level of sensation the distinction exists.

Summary.

Let us conclude this chapter by returning to the text with which it began. Every moment's experience has two elements within it: I meet with some reality, and in that meeting I feel, I bear, and I act. To meet with reality is knowledge. In knowledge is involved on the one hand that kind of recipient activity which we call apprehension: on the other hand there is involved an object known. To the consideration of this object we must now turn.

CHAPTER II

The Distinction.

EVERY name that we pronounce, says Twardowski[1], has three functions; it is the sign of an act of apprehension in the speaker; it names a thing; and it produces a certain content in the mind of the hearer. Meinong[2] says that speech refers to[3] our object and expresses our content. The distinction between act or event of presentation and object presented has already been dealt with. We have now to examine the distinction between object and content.

The basis of the distinction is the fact that the object, in appearing to us, seems never to have come to the end of its powers. No matter how much we know of it there is always more to be known. There is no end to the questions which we may ask of it or to the answers that it may give. There is always some further way in which it may exhibit itself; always some more of its character yet to be shown. It is impossible, therefore, that the whole object should ever be exhaustively contained in our con-

---

[1] *Zur Lehre vom Inhalt und Gegenstand,* p. 12.

[2] *Ueber Gegenstände höherer Ordnung,* p. 189.

[3] *Bedeutet.*

sciousness. Such of it as is so contained may conveniently be spoken of as the *content* of our apprehension.

Object might be said to differ from content as the "subject" of a treatise differs from its "subject-matter." The content is as much as gets into the consciousness; it is all that we are knowing of the object that we know[1]. The content is the present appearance of reality in our consciousness. We have no reason to assume that the appearance must be purely sensuous[2], and therefore the content must by no means be identified with the sense-image as such. Such images generally, perhaps always, constitute part of the object's means of appearing, and thus form part of the content; but the imagery will seldom be the whole of what we are apprehending in the object.

The content is all of the object that at present appears: it is the present expression of the object's character. As to the relation of the object to the whole of its possible contents, and the question whether it should be called their sum or their law or the link between them or the essence behind them, this is the immense and ordinary problem of the nature of substantial reality, and cannot be dealt with here. We shall follow the ordinary custom of using different expressions at different times; and shall know that none of them can express the whole truth.

We must insist that the difficulty in this matter is absolutely nothing else than the universal difficulty of conceiving substance or character or idea, or the general relation of universal to particular. The relation of object to content is not even a special case of the difficulty; it is

---

[1] In just the same sense Dr Stout contrasts an object with what he calls a "presentation" (*Manual*, pp. 58, 59).

[2] See below, section on "Imagery."

the ordinary case; one might almost say the whole case. The relation of content to object is the same as the relation that "what I see" in a misty landscape bears to the landscape as such. One might wish to say, and for many purposes one might conveniently say, that this landscape was the sum-total of all that could ever be seen in it. Yet even this is circular. And it is not exhaustive; for the landscape is more than can ever be seen; it is, for instance, a result and exhibition of geological forces, and it plays a part in history, and it is a factor in the minds of men who build houses in the neighbourhood. Therefore we presently hesitate to say that it is the sum of its visual appearances, and we say instead that it appears or expresses itself in the visual appearances. And then come further problems. Yet this relation, of a thing to what I see of it, is the most ordinary of relations. And the relation of object to content is nothing more recondite than this.

Hence there is danger in all accounts of the relation which do make it appear more recondite; in those, for instance, which take the content to be a copy or a symbol of the object. Twardowski says that it is like a painted landscape, which is not a landscape at all but a picture. This seems to open the door to a whole army of difficulties, and to artificial and unnecessary difficulties; for to have a presentation is a much simpler thing than to make a copy; it is to see. There is danger even in speaking of one special kind of presentation, namely sense-imagery, as a copy, because the word inevitably suggests a reproduction in a different material. When I remember an object and its image comes up, this in a sense is a reproduction, but there is no " material " to change. It is a reappearance; the object presents itself in its habit as it lived.

Any suggestion of a symbolising relation[1] seems still more artificial and unmanageable. How can the one possibly be a symbol of the other, and if it were how should we ever find it out? Unless "cognition" is apprehension *of objects*, the conception is useless for philosophy.

Distinctions of Detail.

The detailed distinctions between the characteristics of object and content which are given by Twardowski and even by Meinong are often not very acceptable for our account of the matter. Twardowski[2] asserts, for instance, that an object of knowledge need not actually *exist*, but that the corresponding content of knowledge must evidently do so. For our view, I actually exist, and my act of apprehension actually happens—I do actually see. As for the content, it and the whole object must exist in some sense that makes it possible for me to see them, but this need not be "actual" existence; for I can see into non-actual worlds. Now beyond this we do not go. If there were something in my consciousness additional to the object it would presumably be an actually existent

---

[1] As made, e.g. by Lipps, *Bewusstsein und Gegenstände*, p. 33, "we might say that the content is a symbol of the object; is a sign of it or represents it." Contrast Mr A. Hoernlé, *Mind*, 1907, p. 86. "I hold it to be manifestly absurd to say that the individual mind, with which psychology is supposed to deal, is conscious of signs only and not of their meaning. On the contrary I regard the consciousness of meaning as primary and fundamental, and the distinction of sign and meaning as a product of reflection." For "consciousness of meaning" I should substitute "consciousness of objects," as being for my purpose less ambiguous.

[2] *Inhalt und Gegenstand*, p. 30.

something, but I see no reason for holding that anything is there. So long as I am actually seeing an object there would seem to be enough to keep consciousness going. What I see is not a piece of consciousness, and it need not be existent in order that consciousness may exist. Consciousness is the process of seeing, and it exists so long as I actually see.

Secondly, according to Twardowski[1], the object and content have different sorts of qualities. A mountain, for instance, is extended even if it is not an actual mountain; but the corresponding content is not extended. Witasek[2] says similarly that a stone is hard, cold and grey, but that my idea of a stone is not.

I am not sure what these authors would say about perception, which of course for me has content and object like other knowledge (as in the example of the landscape above). Is the percept of a mountain extended? or is the percept of a stone grey? The "spirit of language" would probably hesitate a little, but would have not the least objection to saying that we see the one object as grey and the other as extended. Therefore the content of our consciousness, which means the object in so far as it enters our consciousness, is certainly extended and grey. It would appear that the whole difficulty comes from a sort of "introjection[3]," from thinking that the contents of consciousness at any rate, if not the objects of consciousness, must be things that people carry about in their heads. It

---

[1] *Inhalt und Gegenstand*, p. 30.   [2] *Psychologie*, p. 3.

[3] Avenarius, in *Viertelj. f. wiss. Ph.* 18, p. 123, quoted by Munsterberg, *Grundzüge der Psychologie*, p. 22—Psychology is apt to suppose that the tree which a man sees is somehow in him, perhaps in his brain, "Diese Hineinverlegung des 'Gesehenen' u.s.w. in den Menschen ist es, welche als Introjektion bezeichnet wird."

is so hard to be content with their having eyes in their heads. The spirit of ordinary language feels it unlikely that a percept is a thing outside my body in the ordinary world, and is quite sure that an idea is not. Hence, it feels, these must be things "in my mind" as opposed to "in the world," and hence they cannot be extended or grey. It would perhaps be the easiest remedy to say bluntly that my percept is in the middle of the plain five miles off, and that there are no such things as ideas. Contents and objects alike exist outside my body. All that happens is that *I see things*.

The same difficulties, I think, occasion and are occasioned by Meinong's claim[1] that a content, unlike an object, must be *present* and must be *psychical*. I am not quite sure of the meaning of "psychical," but fear that it is meant to rule out "physical"; which of course in my account must not be ruled out. On the other hand, the statement of both Meinong and Twardowski that various contents may correspond to one object and (in the case of universals) various objects to one content, is perfectly sound.

I am embarrassed, but I think not rightly embarrassed, by the reflection that the distinction between content and object has been originated and worked out chiefly by the writers I have been criticising, and that they might claim to be allowed to use their own terms in their own way. They might; yet I only criticise because in so far as they agree with me the distinction seems to me so good and valuable. "Contents" may be admirable tools if we can keep them free from the taint of the old "ideas," and can remember that the things which enter the mind, and which therefore are partly contained in our mind, are the same things that exist outside our body in the ordinary physical world.

[1] *Gegenstände höherer Ordnung*, p. 185.

The Object of Attention.

Should we say that it is the object or the content that is presented or apprehended? Twardowski[1] answers the question by saying that we have a double use of words, comparable to the way in which we speak sometimes of a painted landscape and sometimes of a painted picture. I also should say that the answer depends on our use of words, but my comparison would be very different. For me the question is the same as if we should ask whether we were more properly said to see a landscape or to see as much as we did see of the landscape.

A similar question, " Is it the object or the content to which we *attend*?" is interesting because the inquiry brings out an ambiguity in the ordinary conception of attending "to" anything. Mr Prichard[2] says that we attend not to a mental "presentation" but to a physical thing; which is perfectly true but does not answer my particular question, since for me the content is only the physical thing with the limits of my consciousness imposed. The stream of my endeavour, set towards that thing, is gradually widening those limits of consciousness, and making the content more adequate to the object. Shall we say that I "attend" to what I see within the limits or to the seen object which is not bounded by them? The usage is not fixed, but if a choice is to be made it seems preferable to take the second alternative. We are usually interested not so much in what we can see as in what we cannot yet quite see.

[1] *Op. cit.* pp. 14, 15.
[2] "The Psychologists' Treatment of Knowledge," *Mind*, 1907, p. 42.

Content and Object of Introspection.

It may be urged that at least in introspection and for the general purposes of psychology we attend to the contents of our apprehension, as such. In a sense this is true, for we make the content of a given act of apprehension into the object of another act. Interest and attention are engaged with the question—not " What was the fact ? what was there ? " but—" What did I apprehend ? " We deliberately stereotype the former limits in order to find what we can within them, since our interest lies in finding out what exactly managed to get in. This account accords with Dr Ward's statement that psychology has for its object the whole universe, but the universe as presented to the individual[1]; and it meets, I think, the objection brought by Mr Prichard that "as presented" must mean "as known," and that no science can treat of things in any other way[2]. Generally speaking, psychology is the only science which, instead of expanding the content of a piece of knowledge, stereotypes its limits because it is interested in their shape.

Introspection has for its object the content of another apprehension, but we have no reason at all to say that its own content and object coincide[3]. The untruth of this is

[1] Article on "Psychology," *Ency. Brit.*

[2] *Op. cit.*, *Mind*, 1907, p. 36.

[3] Witasek seems to assert this : "Nur dass bei den Wahrnehmungsvorstellungen von Psychischem der Inhalt mit dem Gegenstande zusammenfällt " (" Zur psychologischen Analyse der ästhetischen Einfühlung," *Z. f. Psych.*, 1901). Of course if content and object are distinguished only because one is supposed to be in the knower and the other outside him, it is fairly natural to expect that an " inner " object will coincide with its content. Yet how can even such an object remain within me when its moment has passed ? Will it not pass out into the world of my past history ? and so be as much divided from its content as ever. I do not mean to accuse Witasek of these confusions.

seen at once if we reflect that introspection, like any other investigation, is usually a process of gradual discovery. Only after careful examination can we discover all the overtones in the sound heard a moment ago, or all the links in the chain of association which has led us to an unexpected subject of thought. Only gradually, that is, does the content become more adequate to the object, which implies that at first at any rate the two were far from coinciding. However we fix our limits, what is within them can develop internally.

The Limits of Objects.

We can no more divide the known world into separate objects, except with the help of convention in places, than we can divide the physical world into separate things. In one sense the whole universe is the object in every piece of knowledge; this is the case at least wherever it is true that to know a bit of the world thoroughly would be to know the whole. We endeavour to expand the content of our cognition until it includes the whole of the object that we wish to know. If this is anything short of the whole universe it will be only because our special interest sets narrower limits to it. We may say that the object is determined by the question we ask, and that the content consists of the answer so far as we know it. If, as is common, we are not quite sure what we want to find out, or if a presentation has come to us apart from any question asked, the limits of the object will so far be undetermined.

The Parallel Case of Feeling.

At no moment, we said, do we find in the presentation-continuum all that might be there. When attention is turned in the direction of any content, that content is ready at once to grow and to set itself out in more various detail and to deepen its relations to everything around. The content expands and becomes more adequate to the object.

Now as it is with the presentation-continuum, so is it with the continuum of desire. The disposition, or tendency, or want, or need, which speaks in a desire, has never in that desire said all that it has to say. No sooner does it gain control over our behaviour than it proceeds to widen and deepen its expression and to write itself out in detail. (This, and not a growth in mere vividness or intensity, is the great change that supervenes when a presentation gains attention or a disposition gains control.) The process may be hindered by the resistance of our materials or of our general environment, just as the development of knowledge may be hindered by the stiffness and narrow-ness of our own intelligence; but otherwise this part of our self expands itself in our life and works itself out to adequate expression and fulfilment.

As for the conception of a disposition and its relation to desires, it is exactly as difficult as that of the relation of an object to its appearances, and no more so. The dis-position, like the object, is a substance which appears, or a character which expresses itself. In one, as in the other, the substance is inexhaustible. On the one side, even when the object of our apprehension is a thing so limited and definite as is a past content of knowledge, even then our content never really becomes adequate to its object, since there is always more that might be found out about it. On the other side, even when the disposition in action is so simple as is that which persists in carrying out a past resolution, even then no actual conation can ever express that disposition completely, for as its materials change it can take an infinite number of different forms. In knowledge we can never come to an end of the smallest part of the universe; in feeling and endeavour we can never come to the end of even the smallest part of ourselves.

The Place of Truth and of Belief.

It only remains to add that just as the sphere of conation is the home both of resolution and irresolution and of right and wrong, so the sphere of contents is the home both of belief and of truth.

The second claim will probably be readily admitted, for if anything is to be true or false it must surely be the contents of our apprehension. Our powers of apprehension are strong or weak, our acts of apprehension are intelligent or unintelligent, our objects are real or unreal, in one sense or another of those words, and our contents are false or true.

The claim that belief also is a matter of content seems at first sight much more difficult to grant, and nearly every realist writer has in fact ignored it, asserting that belief and the strength of belief are qualities not of the content known but of the act by which we know[1]. Idealist

[1] E.g. Meinong, and perhaps Stout, though he speaks of "attitude" instead of "act." See *The Groundwork of Psychology*, p. 3.

writers have usually granted that the modality of a
judgment is a matter of content, but have held that the
psychological variation in degree of belief, the flickering
of belief as it were, is a variation not in content but in
act.   Nevertheless it would seem that in both cases the
difference lies primarily in the content.   In the first case
that content is more or less limited, in the second it is
more or less unsteady: and in neither case have we any
choice in the matter: the content presents itself and
we apprehend.   Consider the following pairs of contrasts,
which include both kinds of variation (modality and
" flickering "):—" Your opinion of his character is clear
and firm; mine is obscure and wavering."   " You believe
that he is certainly innocent, but I am not yet fully
persuaded; I can see only that he may possibly be so."
" You believe his story, but I cannot be sure myself that
it is not a feat of imagination."   " That explanation which
for you is a certainty seems doubtful to me."   " So far as
one can see, he has behaved well;—in that I agree with
you; but I urge that we cannot yet see all."   These
appear to be typical instances of belief and doubt, and
I cannot but consider that in each case the contents
are contrasted.   In the first example the difference of
clearness would certainly be admitted to lie in the contents, and there seems no sufficient reason for putting the
difference of steadiness elsewhere.   In the second example,
one witness apprehends " that the man is innocent," the
other only " that he may be innocent."   In the third and
fourth, the doubter sees a narrative clearly before him, but
cannot yet see whether its connections unite it to the
world of fact or to that of imagination; in this respect his
content of apprehension is as yet undetermined.   In the

fifth example, the evidence which to one man appears to be a proof seems to the other to be less than a proof. " The appearance is different";—what is this but saying that the content is different?

Acts of apprehension with different contents are in so far unquestionably different acts, therefore I do not mean to urge that in doubt and belief the acts are not different. I urge only that the difference lies primarily in the contents. The activity of every apprehension is (as I hold) identical in its peculiar nature as being an activity of reception only, and just this peculiar nature seems to exclude that variation in degree which is supposed to belong to belief. We cannot more or less receive except in the sense that we can receive more or less; and we cannot apprehend differently except so far as what we apprehend is different. Thus, it seems to me, the difference between doubt and belief can involve a difference in act only if it rests on a difference of content.

We shall return to this subject again, and shall be occupied with it at intervals until almost the end of the book.

CHAPTER III

THE FIELDS OF PRESENTATION. I

THERE are apparently at least three ways in which an object can be apprehended. It can be sensed, or imaged, or, in the broadest sense of the word, it can be thought. The relation which these methods bear to one another is by no means a simple one.

There seems no doubt, to begin with, that in all these departments the *object* may be the same. Some objects, it is true, can be presented only in thought and not in sense, but if an object can be presented in sense it can always be presented in thought and can often be imaged.

Secondly, it seems that in these different fields the object is differently presented,—that the *content* differs. It differs considerably if we compare sense with the most advanced thought. As regards sense and sense-imagery, there is always, in the normal case, a difference between the contexts of their contents, and usually some internal difference as well. Few people have visual images as full or as steady as their visual sensations, and in nearly all cases there is a difference in their position and interconnection[1]. Mr Hoernle indeed says[2] that the difference

[1] I neglect for simplicity's sake the important point that most images correspond not to mere sensations but to percepts.

[2] "Image, Idea, and Meaning," in *Mind*, 1907, p. 92.

between sensation and image is "a difference of mode, not a difference of content," but I think he only means to deny that the object (in my language) is different.

Thirdly, it is usual to say that the *act* is different in these different cases. Mr Prichard[1] for instance says, "The act of perceiving is one thing and the act of conceiving is another"; and Witasek[2] even declares that images and sensations differ not in content but in act. This position is very difficult to maintain. It is usually supposed that we confuse sensation and image when their contents become very much alike, and this should be impossible if the acts differed independently of the contents.

A serious objection to the whole theory that sensation of thought and imagery differ in act seems at first sight to arise from the fact that conjunction in one field may produce association in another. It is fairly intelligible (or so we are apt to consider) that to think first of A and then of B should establish a habit of thought-transition, and a tendency to think again of B after we have thought of A. But if to sense is one action and to image is another, then why, when only the sensation of A has been followed by the sensation of B, should we have the slightest tendency to image B after imaging A? And if thinking is a third kind of action distinct from the others, why should linked sensations leave behind them a tendency towards the linking of thoughts, as seems to happen in the case where we can reproduce the argument of a speech that we have heard although we have forgotten the words that were used?

---

[1] "The Psychologists' Treatment of Knowledge," *Mind*, 1907, p. 51.
[2] *Psychologie*, p. 75.

As a matter of fact this objection proves too much.
It must be invalid if it proves that the action involved is
identical whether we apprehend in sense or imagery or
thought; for we have already admitted that the contents
apprehended are different in these three fields, and therefore the acts of apprehending them must in so far be
different in character.   What then is the flaw in the
objection ?   In our present uncertainty as to the details
of association, a believer in absolute differences between
the acts in question might make a very fair case by simply
denying the alleged transference of connections from sensation to imagery or from sensation to thought.   It is indeed
difficult to produce any clear proof of such transference.
One is naturally tempted to instance the reproduction of
a heard tune in auditory imagery, but our opponent is
entitled to answer that such reproductions as often as not
take place in an altered key, with every note changed,
so that the habit-tendency in force cannot possibly be one
which links the apprehensions of separate sounds.   That
is, we have no transference here of sensation-links into
the field of images.   The links which really hold must be
those which bind together our apprehensions of the shapes
of successive phrases.   Now apprehension is a matter
neither of sensing nor of imaging, seeing that the shape
of a phrase is neither a sensum nor an image, but an
" object of higher order."   The act in which we apprehend
it may easily remain identical even though the individual
sensations be changed and even though images be sub-
stituted for sensations.   The habit-connections hold, our
opponent may therefore urge, not first between apprehensions of sensa and then between apprehensions of images,
but between unaltering apprehensions of objects of thought.

Hence, he may say, there is no evidence here for the identity in any respect of the act of apprehending sensa with the act of apprehending images. With our other example of reproducing the argument of a speech it is easy for him to deal in the same way. For we certainly could not reproduce the argument unless we understood it at the time of hearing the speech, and if we admit that we did understand it we are at once provided, as in the case of the tune, with a series of thought-apprehensions which need suffer no change when the individual sentences are altered. Not the series of sensations but the series of thoughts leaves behind it the tendency to repetition of that series of thoughts.

In these cases our opponent's explanation seems irrefutable, yet I am not convinced that a connection between mere sensations cannot in any case give rise to a connection between mere images. The most satisfactory theory in all respects seems to me to be the following: that the activity of apprehension does differ in sensation and imagery and thought, but only because and in so far as the content apprehended is different. If this is true, then a sense-connection may pass over into an image-connection just in so far as the content (the quality of a sound for instance) can remain unchanged. The bare sense-connection could hardly give rise to a connection of thoughts, because it is impossible that sense and thought should have the same content. This appears to me to coincide with the most probable account of the phenomena of association so far as they are at present known, and to be also the simplest *a priori* view. Knowledge will then be apprehension, simple reception, throughout, and will vary only in so far as there is variation in that which is received.

As a matter of language, I prefer to speak in this connection not directly of a difference of act as between the different ways of apprehending, but of a difference of level or field.

Examination of Certain Levels.

Taking our three "levels" without further examination to be those of sensation and sense-imagery and of what in the widest and vaguest sense we call thought (of course this includes far more than one "level" if we proceed to count them), we will spend some time in examining various important points in connection with each of the three.

CHAPTER IV

THE FIELDS OF PRESENTATION. II

A. SENSATION.

ONE of the most interesting questions which can be raised with regard to the sense-level is this : if in sensation as in other forms of cognition a real object is presented to us, what is that object here ?

The question is subtle as well as interesting, and the result of considering it has often been that the existence of any such object has been denied. Sensation has been removed from the line of true presentation, in my sense of the word, and classed as a mere modification of consciousness, which we might use to help us in obtaining information about the real world, but which, as it stood, supplied us with no such information. This opinion has been so strongly supported and is so attractive in many ways, that a special chapter[1] must presently be devoted to its examination; at present I shall refrain from controversy, and only set forth my own opposite view with as much plausibility as I can.

We may conveniently divide our subject into three parts. In the first place, a sensation may fall in the

---

[1] Chap. VI.

margin of our consciousness and remain there, forgotten
as soon as it ceases, and never used in any purposeful
exploration of reality. Secondly, it may be used in the
course of such an exploration ; in an examination of that
physical world which contains our own body and other
bodies outside it. Thirdly, for certain special purposes
we investigate not so much that physical world itself as
what may be called its ways of behaviour with regard to
sense ; it is these investigations which supply us with the
geometry of notes and colours, and with the science of
music as distinct from the physics of sound. Assuming
that in all these divisions a real object is presented to us
in the sensation, we have to remember one warning—that
there will be no profit in any attempt of theory to confine
that object to what enters in the content of the sensation.
In our original distinction between content and object, for
all presentation alike, the object was explicitly not limited
by that portion of itself which at the moment had entered
our consciousness. In fact it was said that the content
could scarcely be conceived as ever being adequate to the
object, because we could never grasp in one act of apprehension the inexhaustible reality of a real thing. In no
presentation, sensational or otherwise, can an object enter
whole.

a. Marginal Sensations.

It is in this first division of the subject that the
strongest reasons seem to show themselves for removing
sensation from the class of reality-presentations altogether.
That which enters in a marginal sensation seems to be so
small and unimportant that it is hard to give it the title

of a real object. On the other hand, we have no right to regard the object entering consciousness as if it were limited by that content which is all that has yet entered. An object is not bound to be small or insignificant because these qualities characterise our knowledge of it.

We must remind ourselves with some care of what exactly was held to determine the boundaries of an object of knowledge. We said, it may be remembered, that in one sense the whole universe might be naturally said to present itself in every presentation, and that, if the object's limits were set anywhere short of this, the fact must be due to the narrow and definite range of our interest. My object of study—that about which I am gradually finding out—is said to be King Arthur's death and not the universe as a whole, only because my interest at present is bounded by King Arthur's death.

Now this leads to a peculiar result in the case where the content has aroused no interest at all. For in this case the limiting factor disappears. The object presenting itself has no other title than reality as a whole. In exhaustive philosophical inquiry at one extreme, and in a marginal sensation at the other, this unlimited universe is the object which presents itself. Width of interest and lack of interest will have the same result[1].

In marginal sensation then, what presents itself can only be said to be the universe as a whole. The content of consciousness is so small and narrow, the speech made is so short, that the object is scarcely specified or defined

---

[1] Compare the way in which the perception of spatial volume may be based either on abundance and variety of positional signs or on their absence; the latter being the case with mist, or darkness, or a snowdrift.

at all.   Reality has entered my life, but has said scarcely
anything.   It has not shown itself yet as a quality or a
relation or a thing.   It has only flashed or resounded.
It has not declared itself as the property of blueness, but
it has been blue to me, has "blued at me." If I will attend
it is ready to say more.

I fear that this largeness of the object in the smallest
of our experiences may seem paradoxical enough, and
yet I believe that the treatment is right.   As for the
paradox, it can be matched on the conative side of
consciousness.   In all desire and action it is true to
say that I as a whole am acting, but very often we
can specify the universe in me which is particularly
concerned; I desire one thing as a member of a college,
one as a private person, I act in a judicial capacity or a
business capacity, the teacher or the student in me is
interested.   Only at the two extremes I cannot thus
particularise myself.   In a high and complete act of will
I "act with my whole heart," I "realise myself"; this is
above particularisation.   In the mere throb of feeling, in
the indefinite emotion, I am below it.   I may be extremely
unhappy without feeling clearly what part of me it is that
has cause to complain.   The thwarted disposition has
spoken, but too vaguely to distinguish itself from the rest
of me.   I say that "I" am unhappy.   The feeling expresses
me, but defines no minor self in me.   And this seems to
be the case not only with actually ignorant feeling but
with all "marginal" feeling.   A disposition cannot define
itself in consciousness until it can so get control of
consciousness as to express itself in desire.   Lacking
attention, then, or lacking control, neither an object
nor a disposition can tell its name; they must appear

merely as reality or as myself. Yet, undefined and unnamed, both have entered consciousness and played a part in life.

Marginal sensation, we conclude, is of all our presentations the one which has the smallest content. It is our first and briefest and obscurest meeting with the reality which is not ourselves. Yet though the content is the smallest possible, the object through lack of determination is the largest; that which presents itself can only be described as the universe.

b. *The ordinary use of Sensations.*

The acuteness of paradox is softened when we turn to those sensations which form part of our ordinary focalised percepts. For here the object is certainly smaller, being limited by the definite interest of the perception; and the content is possibly larger; at any rate if it is true that a sensation becomes more vivid or intense on being brought out of the margin of consciousness. The additional perceptual content of course cannot be included in the content of the sensation as such.

The object is no longer merely the universe at large, but what then is it? As elsewhere, it is whatever further investigation shows it to be, and such investigation normally reveals certain things in a certain situation in the physical world. Sensation is our first and narrowest apprehension of these. My sensations are elements in the content through which a coloured signal lamp, a noisy train, and a bitter evening wind reveal themselves to me. These, I might say, are the objects which present themselves; and the statement would be true and would cover the largest part of the truth. Yet there is more to be said. For though it is these objects that chiefly interest me, yet by themselves they cannot supply the content of my sensational experience. Not the lamp and the wind alone and unrelated express themselves in the green radiance and the freezing touch, but the lamp and the wind in relation to my human body, having its nervous system in working order.

We recognise readily this second factor in the object presented whenever our sensations are found to differ from those of the companion who stands besides us. The sensation of cold for me is sharper than for him, because I have sat by the waiting-room fire whilst he has walked briskly across the fields. The green which I see is different from his because of a defect in my sight; the local signature in the sensations, moreover, is obviously expressive as much of my body's position as of that of the lamp. We recognise the same fact wherever bodily effort is closely bound up with the sensation; what we feel as we struggle homewards is obviously not simply the wind but the pressure of the wind against our bodies. I am nearly always interested in, and attentive to, the outward objects alone, so that these pre-eminently are revealed to me; yet this is not always so. If an instrument is passed over my skin I say that I feel the instrument, but if it presently touches an open wound I am likely to say instead that I feel the wound. What I really feel throughout is of course the contact between the instrument and my body, apprehended first through touch and then through pain. What is presented to me in sensation is always a section of the physical world in which my body is included; but though the outward objects are speedily perceived as

well as sensed, it may be long before my body presents
itself in anything beyond the sensation. It is sensed but
not recognised[1].

c. The peculiar use of Sensations.

This final case is comparatively easy to deal with.
Our interest is narrowly bounded, and cuts off the
sensational expression from the rest of the situation which
thus expresses itself, so that we go on to construct a
science of notes or colours instead of a science of musical
instruments or of physical optics. In this respect our
procedure is of the same kind as that of mathematics,
which cuts off shapes and numbers from the actual objects
to which they belong. The object presented will now be
not a physical situation but only a note or a colour. Here
at any rate the content of sensation might be thought to
exhaust its object, yet of course this does not happen even
here, for sensation cannot tell even so much as that the
tint it apprehends has a special place in a colour-scale.
However definitely we stereotype the limits of a content
in order to make that content the object of a new act
of apprehension, still under that new apprehension the
object will develop internally, and we shall know far
more of it than we did. Paradoxical though it may
seem, even when an object is bounded by a presented
content because our interest is thus bounded, even then
there is indefinitely more in the object than in the content.
The content of the sensation, let us say, was a single note.

---

[1] That is, my *perception* abstracts, expanding one part only of the
content of sense. The object of perception usually excludes the relation
of the external thing to my body, though the object of sensation is bound
to include it. Only part of the sense object, therefore, is usually allowed
to develop itself as an object of elementary thought.

The object also in this case is the same note, but it contains a hundred features that sense could never detect: it is the note of a violin, it is the note G, it is the highest note and the climax of its phrase, it is beautifully produced. All this belongs to the object of sense, yet could not enter the content of sense. Even though a content covers its object it cannot exhaust it.

B. IMAGES.

The problem of images is a curious and difficult one for psychology. How comes it that we can literally see an object that is absent, unhindered by the sight of what is present? How can I hear the wind on a still day, in a manner that prevents it from mingling with the sound of the brook at my feet? This kind of cognition is no higher than sense with regard to the contents that it can apprehend, yet it is superior in being able to dispense with the material presence. The connection with sense is certainly very close, and we speak of an image without hesitation sometimes as the revival of sensation, yet the connection is a mystery in the end.

But the most important question for my present purpose is that of the relation of imagery not to sense but to thought; and this question at present is one of the most controversial in the whole psychological field. The absence of experimental training is a great disadvantage to any one who presumes to enter such a dispute, and forms to some extent a disqualification of the value of his opinion; yet I am unable to avoid holding an opinion on the matter, and a strong one. If psychology is to be consistent either with philosophy or with common sense, it is to my mind bound to recognise that there is a cognition which goes far beyond imagery. I can see no way of describing the actual state of human knowledge unless we admit that our mind can apprehend an infinite number of objects which could never be contained in sensation and which therefore could never be contained in sense-images.

I can conceive no satisfactory answer to Dr Stout's admirable demonstration in *Analytic Psychology*[1] of the extent to which our thought outruns our power of imaging, but some recent experiments have added further evidence. In those conducted by Dr Bühler[2], for instance, his subjects were sometimes asked to state from memory the number of statues on a certain bridge, or the number of colours or figures in a picture. It was found sometimes that the image of the bridge or the picture preceded and suggested the answer, and sometimes that it followed the apprehension of what the number was. The figures seen in the image were sometimes counted, but often the number-knowledge was quite independent of this. More complicated questions, demanding difficult thought on psychological matters, gave even more striking results. Bühler asserts definitely his own conclusion, that thought goes beyond any images which may be present, and cannot be reduced to them or to any other lower form of experience. We cannot even reduce it to consciousness of ability to image, for the subject usually knows what it is that he could image.

[1] Vol. I., ch. 4.
[2] *Arch. f. ges. Psych.* 9 and 12, 1907–8.

Conclusions like enough to Bühler's to serve all my purposes are drawn from their own experiments by J. Orth[1] and by N. Ach[2]. "We find contents of great complexity," says Dr Ach, "where we are conscious of the manifold inter-relations amongst the parts, and where yet these parts receive no adequate representation in speech, and perhaps are not capable of being thus represented....Sometimes we have a lightning-like vision of a content which would require several sentences to express it, and which therefore cannot possibly, on account of its brief duration, be expressed in words. Yet the sense may be given unambiguously, and the remembrance may be clear and definite, without any sensory qualities being discernible in the mental process[3]."

The experiments of Herr Marbe, earlier than any of these, seem to me to lead irresistibly to the same result, though that author does not draw such a conclusion himself[4]. In the course of making a good many judgments and of understanding, or rejecting as meaningless, propositions presented to them, his subjects attested the presence of images and feelings of miscellaneous kinds, but they found no image or feeling whose presence distinguished understanding from non-understanding, or judgment from what was not judgment at all. Sometimes the subject describes his state of consciousness as " knowledge that the given combination of words was meaningless and of the same sort as the meaningless combinations which had been given before," and denies that in all this

[1] *Gefühl und Bewusstseinslage*, 1903.
[2] *Ueber die Willenstätigkeit und das Denken*, 1905.
[3] *Op. cit.* p. 215.
[4] *Experimentell-psychologische Untersuchungen über das Urteil*, 1901.

any image was present except the word "dasselbe" (p. 86).
Sometimes all images are denied: the subject asserts that
his judgment was made "rein reflektorisch": which
Marbe reproduces in a very misleading way as "rein asso-
ciativ" (p. 20). His own expressed conclusion seems an odd
one (p. 91). "We understand a judgment when we know
with what objects it is meant to agree." "Knowledge is
never given in consciousness....To know anything means
to be able to make right judgments about it." "Hence
to understand a judgment means to be capable of making
certain other judgments." If this means, as it seems to
mean, that what is in consciousness is the same whether
we understand a proposition or do not understand it (or,
in other experiments, whether we consider it to be true
or to be false), the assertion appears to me to be absurd.
What can consciousness be if judging and understanding
do not come into it? The difficulty in Marbe's mind, as
in that of other writers, seems to be, How can any
presentation come into consciousness except as an image?
I conceive that the answer is simply, This is what
thought is for. Thought experience, as Bühler main-
tains, is a matter of fact, and it cannot be reduced to
what is less than thought-experience.

This opinion has remained with me stubbornly even
after reading Professor Titchener's recent criticism of the
whole theory[1]. One feels exceedingly diffident in the
presence of such learning as Professor Titchener's, and an
experimental equipment so fine as his, and yet I cannot
see how his account of cognition can possibly work.
Beyond images, he says, "I can bear witness both to

[1] *Experimental Psychology of the Thought-Processes*, 1909.

kinaesthesis and to cortical set, but between these extremes
I find nothing at all[1]." It may be valuable for us to
remember the possibility of extra-conscious factors such
as cortical arrangements. Nevertheless I cannot get
beyond this position:—that if nothing could enter a consciousness except sensations and images, the mind thus
conscious could be debarred from knowing any more than
one thousandth part of what human beings do know.

I am additionally hampered by what seems to me an
ambiguity in Professor Titchener's own expressions. On
page 15 he asserts "What is abstract and general (in a
so-called abstract idea) is not the idea, the process in consciousness, but the logical meaning of which that process
is the vehicle." If I understand this rightly I thoroughly
agree with it, and I should take it to imply that the
"logical meaning" not only of an abstract idea but of the
ordinary idea was something other than a process in
consciousness: certainly something other than an image.
But on page 175 he says, "An idea means another idea,
is psychologically the meaning of that other idea, if it is
that idea's context. And I understand by context simply
the mental process or complex of mental processes which
accrues to the original idea through the situation in which
the organism finds itself." Psychological meaning is therefore apparently different from logical meaning. Here
again, if the contextual processes which form the psychological meaning consist in apprehension of that real object,
concrete or abstract, which forms the logical meaning, I
could accept the doctrine. But the author goes on to give
descriptions which seem inconsistent not only with this

[1] P. 188.

reading of his view but with one another. "The meaning of the printed page may now *consist in* the auditory-kinaesthetic accompaniment of internal speech." "There would...be nothing surprising...in the discovery that, for minds of a certain constitution, all conscious meaning is *carried* either by total kinaesthetic attitude or by words." "As a matter of fact, meaning is *carried by* all sorts of sensational and imaginal processes." "We should probably find that...any mental process may possibly *be* the meaning of any other[1]." I can neither put these statements together nor yet understand how on any reading they can provide for our actual knowledge of the world.

From his protests against the "psychology of reflection," and against the interference of philosophical or epistemological considerations in psychology, I have now and then been inclined to think that Professor Titchener considers this last argument an illegitimate one. I cannot so consider it, nor can I get over the difficulty it puts in the way of a purely sensational psychology. On the other hand, certain of Professor Titchener's objections from the side of introspection seem to me to suggest an unconscious begging of the question. "It may very well be true," he says, "that the thought of diamonds was there before the sound of the word," and that "you know what you want to say" in conversation before the words themselves appear. But what is a thought-of? and what is a knowing[2]? These questions, on the non-sensationalist hypothesis, of course cannot be answered by any analysis of the process into a complex of images : it seems probable that they could never be answered except by a description

---

[1] pp. 177, 178.   Italics mine.   [2] p. 152.

involving constant reference to the object known, as it enters more or less fully and more or less vividly, with more or less complication of associates, into the content of consciousness. But it is just this reference to the object that Professor Titchener rules out[1].

Much of course remains to be done in the discovery of the details of non-sensational cognition. But for my purpose, and I should say for the purpose of any theory of knowledge, its existence must be assumed. That is, I shall assume that whether or not thought is always accompanied by imagery it is by no means bounded by imagery; and that the mind is capable of apprehending directly not only sensuous reality but any reality whatever.

C. THOUGHT.

Let us then admit the existence of a third level of apprehension, or rather of an indefinite number of levels, upon which we may meet with all those objects of know-ledge which cannot enter in sense or sense-imagery. For want of a better general title we must bring all these levels under the name of thought. It is in these regions that we are able to apprehend all "objects of higher order" —shape and position, melody and rhythm, likeness and difference. We find here that meaning or quality in things which is presented to the artist's mental vision, and which by his art he tries to make plain to ours. Here we find invented objects and remembered objects, so far

[1] *Op. cit.* pp. 145–152.

as they go beyond imagery. On these levels, if anywhere, we apprehend our own feelings, activities and dispositions, and those of others. On these levels we can apprehend not only " objects " in the narrower sense but also " objectives" : those "facts" of which the apprehension constitutes both judgment and the cognitive element in assumption. Here we can show forth those connections and identities in things in the showing of which all argument consists. Here, finally, we have that complete grasp of a whole in its parts which sets us above the need of discursive argument.

For all these levels I intend to go on using the metaphor of sight and the terms " present " and " apprehend." (I use the latter, as was said at the beginning, simply as the correlative of the former, and not in any sense connected more closely with its etymology.)   To my mind they describe the facts better than any other terms could do. Judgment, for instance, must come under the general head of apprehension, even if we reserve the name for the apprehension of objects of a particular sort.

Certain Important Presentations.

In our miscellaneous list of thought-presentations three points need particular mention on account of their connection with many controversies.

  a. *Objectives* can be apprehended :—the contents of affirmative and negative judgments. Sense of course can apprehend neither: to grasp them is the peculiar office of thought.

Most writers on the subject, including Meinong and his followers, have seen in the nature of objectives a reason for denying that judgment can fall under apprehension at all. The determination of affirmative and negative, they have said, must belong not to content but to act: but it cannot belong to such an act as apprehension, therefore judgment (and similarly assumption) must be an act other than apprehension. I agree with Mr Bertrand Russell[1] in believing that this claim is based on a confusion. The fact seems to be that there are two distinct kinds of " yes-no determination," of which one belongs to an act of choice and has no special connection with cognition, whilst the other belongs to a cognitive content. The first distinction of yes from no, affecting our act, is seen in the contrast of granting and denying a request. The second distinction, affecting primarily not an act of ours but an object that we know, is shown in the contrast of the presence with the absence of some feature in the object. The first difference, of acceptance and rejection, does not concern us here: the second, which does concern us, qualifies an object in the known world and is itself known, and I see no reason why the knowledge of it should not be described as apprehension.

b. *Connections* of fact can be apprehended. It is of course most important for psychology to recognise that such apprehension exists and constitutes the foundation of inference. For otherwise we have no defence against the popular doctrine that reasonable thought is governed by association.

If we take association to have its ordinary technical meaning of the force of habit in thought, it is evident that

[1] See Mr Russell's articles in *Mind*, 1904, on " Meinong's Theory of Complexes and Assumptions," especially pp. 348–52. For him, however, the apprehension of an objective is not a judgment but an assumption.

a train of good new reasoning can no more be governed by association, generally speaking, than any other purposive activity can be governed by habit in its main lines. Habit may support us usefully in details, but that will usually be all. We find our way to a new conclusion in thinking as we find our way to a new district in exploring a country, not mainly by habit, but by observing the lie of the land and searching out the road.

If association is used in an untechnical sense to cover all kinds of connection of content, then naturally inference is association. But if it is used in its technical sense of habit, then nothing can be more different than the two kinds of connection. Association connects thought-contents by means of making habitual the transition between the respective *acts* of thought. Inference connects contents by means of uncovering the bond that exists between the *objects*. Difficulty comes only from the constant combination of the two processes. We usually remember our multiplication tables, for instance, by the help of true association, but we believe in them on account of inference or of trust in past inferences[1]. Unless it is by confusion and self-suggestion, association is of course unable to found belief[2].

[1] The same combination of two processes, too elementary in this case to be naturally called inference and association, but still of the same kind, is found in the tied ideas of perception. We expect green grass to be cool to the touch because (without being able to argue the point) we believe that the nature of the object grass connects them. But habitual transition probably helps the green to remind us of the cool.

[2] All this, a commonplace in logic, is really not a commonplace in popular psychology. Training-college students, brought up on text-books of " psychology for teachers," will attribute miracles to association with a confidence that might be incredible to a logician who was not familiar with this literature.

c. Other people's minds, with their thoughts and feelings and activities, are apprehended on these levels of
thought. However we come by our knowledge of other
selves, whether by an analogical argument or by some
simpler way, the fact remains that we do know a great
deal of them. When in true thought-knowledge I contemplate the physical world, not only my objects but the
contents of my mind are made of wood and stone. When
I contemplate my friend, the contents of my mind are
"made" of his spirit and his spiritual activity. For this
it is that enters my consciousness and is present to my
thought[1].

Uninferred Knowledge.

As we glance over the kinds of knowledge obtained on
the level of thought, it becomes evident that, even with the
widest meaning of the term inference, not all of them can
be classed as inferential. Such an account would indeed
be impossible, since without infinite regress we cannot
suppose that every piece of thought-knowledge is derived
inferentially from other pieces of thought-knowledge, and
since our sensations, being incapable of apprehending
objectives, are incapable by themselves of supplying us
with any premises for inference. Hence non-inferential

---

[1] I suspect that some readers may find difficulty in accepting this
doctrine, yet it seems to me inevitably true. If the content of knowledge be defined as I have defined it from the beginning, as the thing
known in so far as we are knowing it, then if we are knowing a person
all that we know in him will be content of knowledge for us. I hope
that any difficulty may be partly removed by Chapters VII. and VIII.,
"Defence of the Presentation of Reality in Thought" and "The
Apprehension of Feeling." In any case I cannot see how on my own
lines I can avoid believing in the thesis.

apprehension must occur in thought as well as in sense, and must in fact be of common occurrence. This conclusion is natural enough, [since inference is only a special method for making the features of reality clear to ourselves and to others], and its truth would probably never have been doubted but for an impression that knowledge which claims to be non-inferential must somehow claim to be infallible.

A list of the objects of uninferred knowledge, set forth by Dr Stout in an admirable essay[1], gives first "self-evident propositions," and secondly "pleasures, pains, emotions, desires and sensations, so far as they are being felt or sensed[2]." The list was probably not intended to be exhaustive. One might add for instance our apprehension of images[3]; and also our knowledge of the objects which we *assume*. Shakespeare, having decreed that Cordelia dies, knows without inference that she is dead. Once more, we ought apparently to add one important and interesting example—that of memory.

Meinong has written a valuable paper on this subject[4], and continued the discussion in a more recent book[5]. His arguments may be paraphrased as follows. First, memory does not look like inference. "I was unhappy yesterday" does not seem to be inferred from known facts of to-day. When we say "I must have put this paper in the drawer since it is there now," we are inferring, but we imply

[1] In *Mind*, 1908.

[2] In my view a feeling may be felt without being known, but the discussion of that subject must be postponed.

[3] Of course this is not, as such, thought-knowledge.

[4] "Zur erkenntnisstheoretischen Würdigung des Gedächtnisses" (*Viertelj. f. wiss. Ph.* 1886).

[5] *Ueber die Erfahrungsgrundlagen unseres Wissens* (1906).

"I do not remember putting it there." The case is the same with a judgment made on first waking in the morning, "I feel so unhappy that I know something must have gone wrong yesterday." So far is true memory from resembling an inference from introspection that, as Meinong points out, the very phrase "I remember" is a little unusual and artificial. The typical memory-judgment takes the simpler form, "Such an event occurred."

Secondly, what is there from which we could infer our judgments of memory? There is scarcely one instance of belief in fact which does not itself involve belief in remembered facts. "I noticed yesterday that the peak of the hill has a peculiar shape." This memory-judgment, we may think, could be tested by to-day's sense-perception. Yet how, except by memory again, can we justify the necessary premise that hills do not usually change their shape in the night? Or we may test it by an appeal to our companions' recollection, yet there again we are assuming the validity of recollection as such. Even a purely personal examination of my own memory must use that memory, for all my acts of recollection except one are already past. I must remember what in each case I did remember, if I am to ask whether that remembrance was correct. Finally, any account of memory-judgment which makes it an inference from memory-images falls under the same condemnation.

Our belief in the past, to sum up, does not seem to rest on inference from other beliefs, and when we try to make it so rest we find that we have too few beliefs apart from it for anything to rest on. Memory in general therefore must be added to our sum of knowledge not derived from inference.

D. SUMMARY OF CHAPTER.

This chapter has been of an irregular kind. Taking in turn the three apprehension-levels of sense, sense-imagery, and thought, we have examined in connection with each whatever point seemed most interesting. In the first case, we asked what object could be supposed to present itself in sensation : in the second, we examined the claim of imagery to constitute the whole of our non-sensational knowledge, and decided that there must be a kind of knowledge, called shortly "thinking," which went far beyond imagery : thirdly, we specified certain contents of our knowledge which could only be found on these higher levels of thought, and we noted that some of these contents were matters of immediate knowledge, in the sense not that we were infallible with regard to them, but that we did not obtain them by inference.

Having thus dealt separately with the different species of knowledge, we must now observe the way in which they combine.

CHAPTER V

The Expansion of Presented Contents

WE remarked in our second chapter that a distinction must always be made between what at any moment was appearing in consciousness and what was ready to appear. No manifestation of an object exhausts the object; the latter can always expand its expression and tell us more and more. Not only can the content thus spread and grow, but in a normal attentive mind it tends almost inevitably to do so. And this expansion is not confined to the level or department of consciousness in which the object originally appeared to us; it is likely to involve them all. The touch of a friendly cat in a dark room is likely to call up the visual image of the cat and a good deal of knowledge about it. Every department gives the object room for special manifestations of its nature, and when the expansion is prevented our discomfort may be great. Dr Stout's " anoetic consciousness[1] " is, I suggest, presentation deprived of this tendency to expand. The object shows itself in the presentation-field, but only as a

[1] *Analytic Psychology*, vol. I.

particular grey, with no expansion into "greyness" or into "cat."

In phrases which may mislead, but which if they do not mislead are excellent, such expansion has been called "interpretation," and the matter presented in the higher fields has been said to be the "meaning" of what is presented in the lower. The furry touch has acquired meaning when the presentment is able to expand over all the fields which are necessary to give us an adequate view of "the cat." We are usually a good deal more interested in the higher extension than in the simple view of the object with which we began, and in this rather peculiar but interesting meaning of the phrase the sensation may be said to "stand for" or "symbolise" what follows; to be interesting in a "representative" capacity. Acquirement of meaning means increase of possibilities. The law of the object's nature is able to act more freely and richly; the experience becomes developable; can be rolled out into many others. A small presentation comes to stand for more in the sense of deepening its aspect of promise; we see in it the beginnings of much potential experience.

The word "symbol," however, is always a little dangerous, and it is especially dangerous in the case of downward expansion, for it exposes us to the whole temptation of exaggerating the importance of images. Not only does a sensation spread upwards, but anything presented initially in thought will generally ripple downwards as far as it can go. A cat which we think of cannot usually present itself in sense-perception (though something very like this is apt to happen in a dream where we begin to think or to read), but it presents itself readily in sense-imagery, visual or verbal. Then we are apt to lose ourselves in all sorts of mazes if we begin to speak of this lower presentation, the image, as a symbol of the higher presentation, the idea. For we are led thus to look on the whole appearance as primarily sensuous, making it an image symbolic, an image with a meaning; and then we naturally consider that the symbol serves instead of what is symbolised, and so come to deny or ignore the existence of the primary higher presentation; and by this time the path from psychology to the theory of knowledge is lost amongst chasms unfathomable.

"Streben nach vollen Erleben."

This expansion of the contents of cognition follows from what Lipps has called our "tendency towards full experience[1]." We tend to submit ourselves to the object as fully as possible; to let it exhibit itself in every department of our presentation-field; even, in "Einfühlung," to assume its position and feel what it may be supposed to feel. Sometimes the striving is too strong for the proper maintenance of the boundaries between universes, and the thought merges into a hallucination; but right contemplation also is a making grow. To contemplate is to set the object in a clear field and to let it unfold before us in the contents of consciousness. Where first we found only sense-contents we presently find shape and position and likeness and distinction, and connections with all the world, and relations on which inferences rest. Picturesquely, we say that we think the thing out.

What in this way happens to a presentation on the

[1] E.g. *Fühlen, Wollen, und Denken* 102, and *Bewusstsein und Gegenstände* 100—127.

supervention of thought has a parallel in what happens to an impulse on the supervention of will. The impulse develops and explains itself. It works out into ordered schemes of means and end, into a steady and purposeful way of living, which may be but slightly affected by the dying out of the desire in its old narrow form. The content of conation clothes itself with will as the content of cognition with thought. Or rather, lest the clothing should be taken to be a mere addition from outside, we had better say that in will and thought both contents receive new life, and new and greater power to express the subject in the one case and the object in the other. The condition is that the current of our life should be turned that way; that the object in question should gain attention and that the disposition in question should gain control.

Expansion through Sense and Thought.

No one field of presentation is sufficient by itself to give an adequate view of a concrete object. Sense must if possible supplement thought, and thought must help sense, and all kinds of thought must assist one another. If this is to be done, each of the fields in question must be capable of having reality presented within it, and hitherto we have assumed that this was the case, and endeavoured to describe as well as we could such presentations as seemed to occur.

Nevertheless there exist and have always existed philosophers for whom this assumption has seemed unjustifiable, because they have found in it one or other of two different mistakes. Some have refused it because in their opinion reality could not be presented in sense, others because they considered that it could not be presented in thought. Either of these opinions would evidently have serious consequences for our whole account of knowledge, and therefore it is necessary that two chapters should now be devoted to their consideration. I can scarcely hope to refute doctrines which have gained the adhesion of some of the greatest minds, but I will try to make clear the way in which I differ from each, and my reasons for doing so. It is possible that the result may be that of making plain to more enlightened readers that I have merely misunderstood the writers to whom I shall specially refer; and I should be glad to believe that this was the case.

CHAPTER VI

DEFENCE OF THE PRESENTATION OF REALITY IN SENSE

My representative opponent in this chapter is Dr Stout. And I may as well begin by saying that after persistent and repeated study I am still not quite sure whether he is really in opposition. I think at one moment that we are fundamentally divided, and at another moment that after all he may be only expressing the same thing in a rather different way. The best I can do will be to set forth Dr Stout's account by means of quotations, and then to set forth my own in contrast, whether that contrast be really only one of language or whether it goes down to the roots of our philosophy.

The following quotations from Dr Stout seem to be the most representative that I can find :—

Manual of Psychology, 1901.

p. 134. "Sensations as such...are psychical states. These psychical states as such become objects only when we attend to them in an introspective way. Otherwise they are not themselves objects, but only constituents of the process by which objects are cognised."

Groundwork of Psychology, 1903.

p. 1. " A psychical process is a process forming part of the life history of some individual consciousness. It is some one's experience, and it actually exists only while it is being actually experienced."

pp. 3, 4. " All subjective states are psychical; but not all psychical states are subjective. Sensations in general, so far as they enter into the relation of subject and object at all, fall to the side of the object, and not to that of the subject. When I listen to the sound of a bell, the act of listening is subjective. But the sensation of sound is my object....The same holds good of sensations in general. They are all psychical states. They actually exist only while they are being experienced. But so far as they enter into the relation of subject and object at all, they are objective and not subjective."

p. 37. "Sensations...are psychical objects."

" *Things and Sensations*," in the *Proceedings of the British Academy* for 1905.

p. 8. " We speak of experiencing a toothache as we speak of jumping a jump. To experience a toothache is to experience a certain kind of experience. Such immediacy does not include any distinction of subject and object. The experiencing is distinguished from the content experienced only as colour in general is distinguished from this or that special colour."

" *Are Presentations Mental or Physical ?* " in the *Proceedings of the Aristotelian Society*, 1908–9.

p. 235. " We must regard dream apparitions as psychical or mental existents. But, in this respect, we can draw no essential distinction between dream presentations...and the presentations connected with the perception of actually existing physical things."

p. 241. "Presentations certainly are not specific qualities of conation or attention ; neither are they modes of cognition, if by this is meant the mental act or state of our being aware of something in distinction from the something of which we are aware. But the real question is whether mental existence is confined merely to consciousness in this sense....There is nothing in (Mr Alexander's argument) which has any bearing on my contention that there are certain existents so connected with conation and feeling as to form with these part of the single system which we call an individual mind."

p. 245. "Doubtless all emotion involves conation and feelings of pleasure and pain.... But these elements are so blended in a continuous unity with organic sensations that it seems quite arbitrary to contrast them as subjective with the organic sensations as objective....Sensations, then, may be, in the proper sense, *subjective*."

Now in contrast with these opinions my own account stands as follows :—

Nothing exists except myself and the rest of the world. My existence takes shape in action ; in part of this I express myself against the world, in the other part the activity is receptive and the world expresses itself against me. In this forth-going and incoming, this expression and apprehension, my life consists. That which I receive and apprehend is the world of reality. My presentation-field of objects is part of this world, and lies chiefly outside my body. The *content* of my apprehension is also chiefly outside my body, consisting of just so much of the world as I apprehend.

Nothing enters my life except on the one hand my own activities (impulses, likings, creatings), and on the other hand so much of the real world as presents itself to me. The content of sensation is not an activity of mine. Therefore it forms part of the world of reality. If it be asked how it fits into that world, and what relation it can possibly be supposed to bear to an abiding physical object, I will only say that reality is already bound to fit together so many odd things, such as physical objects, laws, qualities, relations, powers, situations, and events, that it can scarcely make much objection to including the contents of sensation as well. For guidance, however, we may note that the latter's immediate connections will be with a part of the physical world which includes that object I call my body.

My mind can contain the whole universe, yet there is no room in it for anything which is not either a part or act of my self or else a part or act of my not-self. The act of sensing, like all my acts, belongs to me, but what I sense does not. No " modification of consciousness " and no " psychical object " can escape the alternative, for there is no room for anything between me and the world with which I meet.

The Sensum.

What really concerns me is to distinguish sensation from feeling on the one hand, and to make it a possible starting-point for thought on the other. In order to obtain these ends, it seems to me necessary that we should do what many thinkers strongly object to doing,—distinguish between the sensum and the act or event of sensing it. The latter is not important here : it may be called an act of recipience, or in the case of marginal sensation at any rate it may be thought worthy of no better title than "event" of recipience: so small may be the activity involved on the part of the apprehending mind. What is important is the sensum, the content received. It appears to me necessary to insist that the event of sensation is the event of the entrance of an element into consciousness, in just the same way as is the event or act of thought. I urge that to give up this is in the first place to lose the distinction between sensation and feeling, and in the second place to make the super-vention of thought, which admittedly has an objective content, exceedingly difficult to explain. We will take these points in turn.

Sensation as Distinguished from Feeling.

Psychologists have usually (though not always) taught that sensation is an experience distinct in kind from conative experience and from feeling in the technical sense. Dr Stout himself, as I understand him, teaches this doctrine[1]; Dr Ward certainly teaches it. Now if the distinction is to be made, I can see no other such natural and fitting way of describing the difference as to say, that sensation is an experience of reception whilst the others are experiences of response. In sensation, we should say, an objective element enters consciousness: feeling and striving-experience are the subjective elements in which I respond to what enters, and express myself as against the world. In elementary life, or with distracted atten-tion, I naturally do not think about myself or about the

[1] E.g. in a very interesting article on the activity-experience, in *The British Journal of Psychology*, Vol. II. July, 1906.

world, nor do I take any notice of the difference between the two sorts of experience. That distinction between self and not-self which leaves my own body on the not-self side is of so little practical importance, that it is long indeed before I come to recognise it. All this I grant, for it does not touch the ordinary doctrine that sensation is different from feeling whether the difference be noticed or not, nor my own claim[1] that the difference, whether we know it or not, is the difference between recipient and responsive experience. Dr Stout, in one of the passages with which my opinions seem to conflict[2], considers the case of a spectator at a football match who unconsciously imitates the movements of the players, so that movement-sensations blend with the impulsive and emotional elements in his sympathetic excitement. Is it not absurd, the author asks, to say that the sensations (in my terminology the sensa) are present as objects whilst the other elements are not? It seems to me really not absurd, but the most natural way of describing that difference in the nature of the elements which, whether or not it is noticed, we admit to exist.

I am willing to accept as typical of sense-experience an instance of it to which Dr Stout often appeals: the instance of physical pain. This, with its distinction from the feeling and striving which it calls forth, seems to me an instance peculiarly suitable for my own exposition. Physical pain, so far as I can see, is emphatically objective. It is not a way of experiencing but a thing that we experience. It comes to us, comes upon us. We are not "in" it as we are in our hatred of it or our struggles to escape from it: we are opposed to it: under it. I know that when

---

[1] Which I take to be practically the same as Dr Ward's.
[2] Arist. Soc. 1908–9, 244.

we reflect and introspect we may use much the same phrases as these about some impulse or disposition which we separate from our main self: but to do this we must reflect, must turn round. Surely no such reflection is required in the case of pain. No part of ourself is in it: it is altogether something inflicted upon us. It is not a way of loving or hating: it is something that we hate. The knowledge of the cause of pain and the endeavour to remove it comes indeed only later. What is primitive is the struggle against, the incredulity towards, the writhing endeavour to escape from, not the cause of the pain but the sensed pain itself.

In the case described we are attending to a sense-content, and it would seem that we attend to it without performing any task so elaborate as that of introspection. Just this, according to the doctrine I support, shows the difference between sensation and feeling. Feeling and impulse cannot be attended to except by introspection and reflection : their tendency as they grow in force is not primarily to gain attention but to gain control over our inward or outward behaviour. But when we struggle against pain, or listen to a musical note, or enjoy the colour of a buttercup, we attend to a sense-content without any turning of our attention inwards, such as occurs when we attend to our dislike or our enjoyment. This is what I mean by urging that sense-contents are objective from the first. What is thus claimed for a content in the focus of attention must be claimed similarly for a marginal content. Sensa, in a word, must be looked on everywhere as objective elements in consciousness, in contrast with the subjective elements of feeling and impulse : or else another distinction must be proposed between these two kinds of experience.

Sensation as Leading to Thought.

My second plea is this: that if the objective, presentative, and "received" character of sense-contents be given up, it becomes very difficult to explain the transition from these to the contents of thought, which are usually admitted to be objective elements.

If the cognition be taken to begin in sensation as in an "immediate unity" of subject and object, and if this means not only that no distinction between subjective and objective is yet recognised by the sensitive subject but also that no such difference is there, the question arises how we ever come to make the distinction, or discover that object world which we know in thought. "Why should thought refer a 'modification' of the individual consciousness to something which is not a modification of the individual consciousness but exists independently of that consciousness[1]?" Lipps accounts for the procedure by an ultimate and irreducible "instinct[2]." Dr Stout, in his account of anoetic consciousness[3], leaves the step unexplained, and explicitly conceives the possibility of a sentient creature which should never be led to take it. There is surely less difficulty in the whole account if we suppose that what thought has to do in supervening on sensation is not to refer to an object or to surround with an object something that is in no sense objective, but only to turn a very small and narrow objective content into one that shall be wider, deeper and richer.

What I desire therefore is to treat sense-contents as

[1] Dawes Hicks, *Arist. Soc.* 1905–6, p. 296.

[2] *Das Wissen von fremden Ichen*, pp. 694–7.

[3] *Analytic Psychology*, vol. I.

I have treated thought-contents: to consider them as objective; as presented, apprehended, received: and as forming the content of our first glimpse of what presently reveals itself as the physical world. Sense-contents like thought-contents may be called psychical with a meaning which does not exclude many of the latter from being also physical: for all mental contents exist in my mind, and the whole universe exists there when I embrace it in thought. Sense-contents like thought-contents often receive little attention, for our attention usually flows through and past what we already know of the object towards that which we do not quite know. Sense-contents have "existential presence[1]" inasmuch as they *are there* and exist before us, are present with us: but this gives them no greater nearness and no less objectivity than is possessed by thought-contents, which also are present with us. In short, in sense and in thought alike we apprehend an object which is presented.

Do Sense-Contents belong to the Real World?

I believe all this to be true, yet for most forms of metaphysics one evident difficulty remains. Granted that in sensation we apprehend a presented content, has that content any claim to belong to the real world? Does not the existence of a sensum depend on the presence of my sensitive self? Is it not therefore inserted by my own mind into that world which is truly presented in thought alone? The answer cannot be simple.

To begin with, it must be said that anything which can be presented has according to my definition some sort of reality. It is able at least to be apprehended: it comes

---

[1] Dr Stout's term.

before us and upon us: we have so far to reckon with it: it forms part of the circumstances of our life. I accept Dr Stout's comparison of sensations with dream-images, which for me are still presentations of reality, though that reality lies far away from the physical world, "draussen im Fabelland." Every presented object has as much reality as enables it to be presented: what further reality it has, and of what sort, are matters for further investigation.

In the case of sense-presentation we have already examined in part what that further reality is. In the ordinary case, we decided, the object presented in sense was most naturally determined as being a certain part of the physical world in which my own body was included. What I feel is the wind against my face, what I see is a forest from which ether waves pass to my eye. Further investigation of the sensum may bring me information both about the forest and about a colour-blindness in my retina. So far one might say simply that the object presented was this complex part of the physical world, and certainly real.

But from the point of view of ordinary realism and ordinary science the difficulty of course is still to come. Granted that the object presented in sense is the one described above, still this remains—that just that part of the object which enters in the sense-content is a part which, when it is not so entering, does not exist at all. The physical world is presenting itself, is exhibiting itself before me, but the exhibition is a special one for my benefit. The relation is very subtle; these contents must not be said to be created by apprehension, seeing that apprehension can create nothing; it is just that my presence gives the world its opportunity, and, my conscious life being there, other bodies combine with my body to flash a sensum into that life. The buttercup explodes in yellow; the sky salutes me with blue; the vexed nerve not only thrills but stings.

The mystery of these objects, which somehow depend for their existence on the presence of an apprehending person, and which yet cannot without absurdity be supposed to be created by his recipience of them, is undeniably great; yet it seems fair to conjecture that some of it would be removed if we understood better how sensation came about, and knew the whole relation between body and soul. Meanwhile I urge that there is nothing in the mystery, great as it is, to force these objects out of line with other objects. For the purposes of psychology and philosophy, if not of physics, they are simply very short-lived parts of the real world.

We have to claim, in short, that the peculiarity of the nature of sense-contents is not of importance for this particular point in our theory of knowledge. If these contents are presented and if they are real, then we have all that for the purpose of the present chapter we require. The nature and origin of their reality is indeed most important for metaphysics, but for our present purpose it seems irrelevant. The object which exhibits itself in sense must indeed be more complex than we had hitherto observed : apparently it must consist not only of bodies in connection with a living body, but of all these conjoined with a mind. This may lead us perhaps to look more carefully into the apparent simplicity of other objects. But for the present my end is attained if I have been able to make it apparent that even in sensation reality is apprehended.

At all events I can make my view no clearer than this, and can only hope in the end that Dr Stout does not really disagree with it.

CHAPTER VII

DEFENCE OF THE PRESENTATION OF REALITY
IN THOUGHT

ACCORDING to the opinion criticised in the preceding chapter, the contents of sense are too near to us to be presentations of an objective reality. According to the opinion now to be discussed, the objects of thought are too far removed from us to be presented at all.

The opinion now in question is in one way more difficult to discuss than the former, because usually it is rather assumed than explicitly set forth. It comes up again and again in the best philosophy, and yet I cannot believe at present that it is anything but a remnant of the fallacy of introjection and of the obsession of representative ideas. What I oppose is the constantly-recurring tendency to believe that only in sensuous experience are we in contact with the real world. The sense datum, it is continually supposed, is all that is " given " to us, and round it we have to make a " construction " of our own. Then, by mere force of assertion apparently, we are held to " identify " this construction with the real world which, except through the hole of sense, we cannot reach.

Now the chief point of which we must remind ourselves is that reality in the general sense is simply what does in any way present itself to us. It is a fact of experience that in all cognition and not only in sense we have something before our eyes, something given in the sense that no choice of ours has shaped it, and in the sense that it does not express ourself as our desires and impulses express ourself. It is our material, a circumstance of our life. What I mean by reality is the substance of all such appearances, and belongs in no way uniquely to sense-experiences. What I mean by the real tower is not only that which I see in the distance but that which I expect, intellectually, to overshadow me when I approach, and that of which I remember the erection and could state the height and conjecture the purpose and reason out the relations: I mean that which in all these ways I actually know. I remember and reckon on and describe the tower, and not any construction of mine which I identify with the tower. For by the name I mean nothing more remote than what in all these ways appears to me. Thus by the very force of words reality is presented not only in sense but in thought.

Inattentively at first, I hear a noise. It strikes me, comes before me, is an object to me. As I turn my attention that way, I find more in this object than I found at first. It shows itself not only as a noise but as a musical noise, as a tune, as the tune of a well-known song, as produced by a particular composer, as well or badly rendered. These are all aspects of the real tune, and not, in the natural sense, of a construction of mine. In all these ways the reality presents itself to me. So also is it with a bodily pain; and with a physical thing which I touch or see: and with objects such as those in the world of mathematics, which mere sense can never apprehend. So also with a human being whom I learn to know.

"But only through sense," it may be said, "have we any guarantee that the object in question is really present with us." Sensation is apparently a guarantee that the object, or effluences from the object, or waves of ether which have lately left the object, have the moment before come in contact with our body. But why should that involve for the object any unique privilege in the way of being now in our mind? Let us pause a moment to examine the meaning of presence to a mind.

There appear to be two methods which may help us to realise this meaning. One is the pushing of our categories one step up; the consideration of the universe for the moment not as substance and quality but as law and expression. A real thing, whatever else it may be, is the method, or necessity, or law, in a group of events. The laws of its nature govern the behaviour of other objects in relation to it and our own experience in respect of it. The number five is a knot of such laws; the constitution of a country is another more complex and far-reaching group; a beech-tree is a third; a man is a fourth. Now "presence" under this category can only mean the actuality of government by the law-group in question; a thing is present wherever the laws of its nature rule. The category of substance seems inevitably to carry with it some association of restricted position in space or time. A substance, we feel, cannot be here if it is somewhere else; it cannot be now if it was once and has ceased to be. Therefore if we cognise such a thing, we think, we are cognising what is away from us, and our knowledge of it must be round-about; what is present with us cannot be the real thing but must be something else, perhaps an idea. But under the category of law an object is present wherever the laws of its nature rule, and that is the only meaning which presence has. "I see Birmingham" means that the nature of Birmingham is expressing itself in my perceptual experience, governing the happenings there ; and the contemplation of a thing in memory, in imagination, or in the most elaborate thought means exactly the same kind of fact. In all of these that law which is the object is *there*, for it works, and there is no other meaning for the presence of a law. Hence it is literally true to say that the past or the future can be " present with me," or that the friend I think of has " entered into my thought " or has been "much in my mind." I can no more think of a thing which is not there within my thought than I can obey a law which is not obeyed. What is presented to us in any field is quite truly and literally in our presence, and what is only presented in thought may be "nearer than hands and feet."

The second method is to reflect that we really do not keep our minds inside our heads, or that, if we do, at any rate the mind's eye can see through the skull. The notion that we have direct apprehension in sensuous experience only is surely, I urge, a mere remnant of the belief that the mind lives inside the body, joined with the undeniable truth that an external object's influence can penetrate the body only by stimulating the sensory nerves. When once we give up this idea, what meaning can there be in "reaching the mind" other than simply "being apprehended"? That is present to the mind which is there before it ; I can no more think of a thing which is outside thought than I can see a thing which is out of sight; and mental vision is not hindered by distance in space or time or even by the separation of its object from the world of fact. Or if we use the phrase "*in* the mind," then our mind is capable of putting itself forth to embrace the whole universe.

Knowledge Inferred and Uninferred.

Some of the chief obstacles in the way of believing that thought brings us into contact with reality seem to have been found in connection with inference. Where any thought-knowledge has been admitted to be uninferred it has often been admitted also to involve the real presence and immediate vision of its object; but it has seemed much harder to admit this of inferential thought. This has come about partly, I think, on account of the ambiguity of the phrase "immediate knowledge." Knowledge that is non-immediate in the historical sense of having been reached by means of other knowledge was thought to be also non-immediate in the epistemological sense of being out of touch with its object. The other cause seems to have been the tendency to describe inference as construction. Inference, like all apprehension, is certainly an act, and often on account of its difficulty it is an energetic and strenuous act, but still, like all apprehension, it is a recipient or exploratory and not a creative act. In it, as in the simplest vision, I am completely submissive to the reality that I meet and do no more than trace the outlines which are to be found in it. This fact is only disguised by the way in which the recipient activity is continually helped and guided by a separate and exceedingly interesting *creative* act—the construction

of hypotheses. Hypotheses are nothing at all but suggestive pictures and guiding lines, yet so useful are they,
and so constantly do we find reality projecting through
the picture we have drawn, that it is hard for us not to
suppose that picture and substance have blended into
one, and so to think that we have partly constructed that
which in real believing inference, not in hypothesis, stands
before our eyes.

Objects of Higher Order.

A different hindrance has beset some philosophers,
arising from the tradition that what is given must consist
only of simple or "foundling" and never of "founded"
contents. Anything in the way of a relation or of a
combination form has been supposed to be contributed by
the apprehending mind, and therefore to be no part of
presented reality. Now, as we said, with the question of
the nature or of the creation of reality we have in this
book nothing to do so far as we can avoid it. It may be
that the object presented to us does in some cases,
possibly in all cases, include in some way a part of our
own mind. Nevertheless reality is able to include that
mind, and such presentation would still be the presentation of the real. Whether or not the founded content
exists by the help of our mind, it certainly is not created
by our recipient apprehension of it. It stands the test
of reality in that it behaves as real: in that it stands
over against us and dictates and is dictated to us: in
that we can reckon on it and have to reckon with it.

Professor James on Conception.

The philosophy last quoted has been vehemently opposed in recent years by a brilliant champion, maintaining the immediate presence of the real object in contents of higher order. It seems strange that this champion should himself become on yet another ground the opponent of the presentation of reality in thought. He is still for some reason so possessed by the tradition of separating thought from immediate knowledge, that, in order to preserve our power of knowing them immediately, he seems disposed to hand all the higher-order contents bodily over to sense.

Radical Empiricism asserts, says Professor James, "that relations between things are just as much matters of direct particular experience as the things themselves[1]." "The great obstacle…is the rooted rationalist belief that experience as immediately given is all disjunction and no conjunction, and that to make one world out of this separateness, a higher unifying agency must be there[2]." "Intellectualistic critics of sensation insist that sensations are disjoined only. Radical empiricists insist that conjunctions between them are just as immediately given as disjunctions are[3]." I am not quite sure who the intellectualistic critic is, having failed to find any statement quite so bad as this in the works of the arch-enemy Green: but that does not much matter. My own position is as follows. (1) Relations of all sorts are given as their terms are given; in the sense that when we look for them we find them, that their nature is fixed by no choice of ours,

---

[1] *The Meaning of Truth*, xii, xiii.   [2] *Op. cit.* xiii.
[3] *A Pluralistic Universe*, p. 280.

and that they are objects presented to us. (2) They are usually not given quite so immediately in point of time as are their terms; we have to look a little more carefully into what is before us. (3) When relations are presented, whether they be conjunctions or disjunctions or any other kind, they are presented not in sense but in thought. There is no meaning in the distinction at all if sense is to be supposed capable of grasping these[1].

General Objectivity of Objects of Thought.

On the whole subject, then, I agree with Professor Alexander[2]. " The difference between what is revealed in sense and what is added in interpretation is solely a matter of the method of the revelation. We are always by one method or another seeing things themselves."

It follows, to my mind, that I must object to the other metaphor according to which thought manipulates reality, though Prof. Alexander in the same paper uses it alternately with that of sight. It follows in the same way that when Green speaks of " what may indifferently be called a constructive act on the part of the subject, or a manifestation of itself on the part of the object," I should strongly prefer the second phrase[3]. Similarly I should avoid Dr Bosanquet's description[4]. " ...This determinate reality, which the individual has constructed by identifying significant ideas with that world of which he has assurance through his own perceptive experience."

---

[1] For further examination of Professor James' position see appendix to this chapter.

[2] *Arist. Soc.* 1909–10.   [3] Green's *Works*, vol. I. p. 387.

[4] *Logic*, vol. I. pp. 3–4.

"Perception is his point of contact with reality as such."
It is only with caution that I should use Herr Rickert's
very suggestive description of knowledge as obedience to
an imperative; caution being needed on account of the
suggestion of "construction" even here. If we are careful
always to think of the imperative as "see me thus,"
"read me thus," and not as "make me thus," the description may be used to excellent purpose[1]. Finally, there is
a danger even in the useful term "Vorstellungsproduk-
tion," employed by Meinong's school[2]. We should all
agree that the act of apprehension was "produced" and
that the founded object which we apprehend was not
produced by the apprehension but founded in reality.
But I should wish to make it specially plain that the
content of cognition was not produced either, since for
me it is simply a part of the whole object; that part
which in thought-apprehension we come newly to see.
Our coming to see it may be mediated; our seeing it
is not.

The objects of thought, then, are real objects, not
constructed by us but given to us; they are materials
and circumstances; they are "hard" facts, which we
"face"; in them we meet with the solid objective world.
We construct nothing; the effort required is only that of
focussing and guiding our sight, and perhaps of seeing in
the dark. Reality lies before us on all levels of presentation and whichever way we look. If we only see it
"through a hole[3]," at all events the hole is nothing worse
than the pupil of our eye.

[1] Rickert, *Gegenstand der Erkenntniss*, p. 66.
[2] E.g. Ameseder in *Gegenstandstheorie und Psychologie*, p. 487.
[3] Bradley, *Principles of Logic*, p. 70.

Note. I may add here once for all that I find no reason to believe in any kind of knowledge which would be superior to the presentation of reality. It has been held sometimes that with perfect knowledge the object would cease to be presented to us because it and we had become one. With regard to this we may find some help again in the substitution of the category of law for that of substance. When reality is looked upon as a substance, odd associations of physical grasp and resistance and strain seem to enter into our thoughts about knowledge. We picture the subject and object as somehow interlocking and pulling each other close, and incline to think that for perfect knowledge they would have to coalesce and become one. But with the category of law this tendency vanishes. The better we know an object, the more elaborately and freely and variously do the laws of its nature express themselves in our experience, but there is no tendency for their field of show to come any nearer. As the mists clear away, the landscape only becomes more and more evidently something which is not the spectator; and perfect knowledge would surely be only a clearer apprehension of the presented.

APPENDIX TO CHAPTER VII

PROFESSOR JAMES ON CONCEPTION

IT is related in the biography of Clerk Maxwell that from early childhood his interest in the mechanism, the " how," of any object was always the first thing with him. "What's the *go* o' that?" he would ask continually. And no mere general answer would content him. "What," he would ask, "is the *particular* go of it?"

This is the search for conceptual knowledge in one of its simplest forms, but it provides a convenient symbol and metaphor for all such search. The endeavour to conceive has usually been deemed an innocent habit in the philosopher, natural or moral, and Professor James's prohibition of the habit seems at first sight like a command to the inquiring boy, "Go back and look at the thing, but refrain from thinking about it." Why are we to be snubbed in this way? I can not help thinking that Professor James is misled, for one thing, by his own matchless power of metaphor.

It is seldom fair to cross-question metaphors, and Professor James's are so vivid and delightful that one is not tempted to cross-question except when, as in the present case, they lead us to quite specially inconvenient results. But when the inconvenience makes one look back, his conception-metaphors seem to me to be really puzzling from the first. We "lay hold of our experiences by" concepts, he says; we string reality on them; they are extracted samples, or photographs. "To understand life by concepts is to arrest its movement, cutting it up into bits as with scissors[1]." I can only say that I don't think I do anything of the sort, and I don't see how it is done. "Concept" must mean either an act of conceiving or a content conceived. For me, the first is a process or event, and therefore neither a string nor a pair of pincers. The second is an element in presented reality, and that again is not a string, but a current or a nerve—a real thing seen.

It is ill to contend in metaphors with a master of metaphor; yet my way of expressing the facts surely avoids the difficulties of the other way, and therefore suggests that they are difficulties of allegory only. In my account, sensation gives us our first and most elementary seeing or feeling of the experience-stream. The rest— perception and conception and their like—are "seeing what," "seeing how," "seeing into"; they are the unfolding of the bud; the epiphany of the rainbow in the heart of the sunshine. The first shimmer of the stream's surface grows as we look at it into the crumpled silver tissue of crossing ripples and patterned gleams, and deepens into levels whence bubbles rise, and undercurrents that crease the surface above and stir the sand below, and all "the light and sound and darkness" of the stream's heart. This it is to conceive. We come to see not only the glint of the stream, but the make of it, "the go of it." And I no more substitute my concepts for sense-reality than I substitute the undercurrents or the shaping bed for the flash of the surface. Nor do I ever assert that either alone can give the whole truth.

[1] *The Hibbert Journal*, April, 1909, p. 568.

I have two quarrels with Professor James's moral of " back to sense."

1. If words are to have any ordinary meaning, he is surely attributing to sense-experience a richness which it cannot have till thought supervenes. It is after all literally true, as Mill and Berkeley teach us, that with the eyes of our body we can not see a man, nor a stream either. We are so much used to extending the meaning of " sight " that perhaps illustration from touch and hearing will impress the truth better. Think of the poverty and barrenness of a succession of touches in the dark, which we can not read off, or interpret, or recognise. Or think of the ear assailed by a continuous meaningless clash of instruments. The listener's " whole experience " is altered, we say carelessly, when he realises at last that five familiar tunes are being played at once. Perhaps it is, but " sensation " is just our name for *the element which is supposed unaltered.* In so far as the experience changes, it is something more than sense. Relations, says Professor James, are " just as integral members of the sensational flux as terms are[1]." True, for neither terms nor relations, neither notes nor tunes, were " given " us in that clash and blare. They were there for the finding, but it was not sensation that could find them. What is secret in sense gives up its secrets in thought. " Intellectualistic writers on sensation insist that sensations are disjoined only. Radical empiricism insists that conjunctions between them are just as immediately given as disjunctions are[2]." Both are " immediately " given, I agree, but not in sense. Confined to sense, we know sensations neither as disjoined

[1] *A Pluralistic Universe*, p. 279.
[2] *Op. cit.* p. 280.

nor as conjoined. Such terms and such relations are revealed when we open our eyes wide enough to see them.
" Pure sensation," for such a writer as Green[1], is surely the
unreachable limiting case of experience accepted without
any inspection ; with our eyes narrowed to a thread's
width; with the given confined to the one field and for-
bidden to expand or reveal itself in other fields. Hence
we have neither " One, and then two, and then three," nor
yet " one, with two and three," but only " one, one, one,"
each forgotten as it passes; or rather it is "thus, thus,
thus"; or, still more, it is " thu-u-u-u-s-s-s-s—" to the end
of the chapter. It is a buzzing which must not expand
into " bee."

2. " The immediate feeling of life solves the problems
which so baffled our conceptual intelligence[2]." Not at all ;
it sets them. Let us grant to Professor James that in one
sense of the word we are " given " all sorts of things as
" integral members of the sensational flux," just as we
are given Mr Chamberlain in a puzzle picture; still the
problem is to find them. We have experience folded ; the
problem is to unfold it. The " feeling " gives us the going
thing; conceptual intelligence seeks for the go of it. The
stream runs and shines; but what is that running ? How
do the currents turn and cross and enfold one another ?
It shines, but what is *in* the shine and the blue ?

It would appear that in this matter Professor James has
misunderstood Mr Bradley's complaints. Mr Bradley, I

---

[1] I agree with Professor James in objecting to Green's speaking as if
our own " combining thought " created relations instead of finding them ;
as if it "did something" to sense experience, instead of finding in it what
sense cannot find.

[2] *A Pluralistic Universe*, p. 260. *The Hibbert Journal*, p. 574.

take it, stands with us by the stream of experience, and we indicate to him certain elements, and movements, and directions, and eddies, which we seem to make out in its flow. " Such and such relations, such and such attributes; such natures of time and space." Mr. Bradley's comment is, " A very slovenly piece of work. If those two currents are on one level, as you say, how can their crossing look like that ? How can the eddy you trace in that corner throw such a shadow on the sand ? Your scheme is right in its main lines, perhaps, but in some ways it is shamefully scamped and muddled. You must learn to see better than this." To which Professor James replies, " But the stream does run."

None of us, surely, are denying the fact of experience. The instruments, we all admit, are blaring in our ears. We, common-sense philosophers, have resolved the noise fairly satisfactorily to ourselves, into our five familiar tunes. Then comes Mr Bradley to torment us. "Are you sure," he says, " that these are really the tunes you hear ? It occurs to me that not one of them can be exactly as you maintain. How can this and that conjunction come in ? How can this particular dissonance possibly be rendered in that way ? Are you right in reading it as five tunes at all ? " When we are thoroughly bewildered with this teasing, Professor James comes to reassure us; and he says, " Thought finds impossibility in tasks which sense-experience easily performs[1]." " With a world of particulars, given in loveliest union—the ' how ' of which you 'understand' as soon as you see the fact of them, for there is no how except the constitution of the fact as given— he asks for some ineffable union which, if he gained it,

[1] *A Pluralistic Universe*, p. 256.

would only be a duplicate of what he has already in his full possession[1]." "Never mind the tunes; there is a great deal of noise going on."

One must confess that Mr Bradley exposes himself rather recklessly to having his point missed, on account of the unexpectedness of his transition from "appearance" to "reality." We know how in a sunny brook the eddies cast trembling but stationary shadows on the sand at the bottom; and it is often easier to see the shadow than to find the knot or crumple which is the eddy itself—much easier than it is to see the run of the water in the knot. Now Mr Bradley, after tormenting us about our careless reading of the make-up of the brook, quite suddenly gives up any attempt to help us with it, and drops down to this fixed shadow-scheme at the bottom. "Somehow," he says, "to cast these shadows, the real water-currents must be thus and thus, though we cannot see how they manage it." But the spectator, seeing the speaker's eyes so abruptly turned from the body of the stream to its bed, concludes that in Mr Bradley's opinion the stream does not exist. "For this philosopher," he concludes, "there is only the surface and the bed; appearance and reality; a fleeting veil of gleams above a stretch of patterned sand."

There are three truths and three corresponding false-hoods in Professor James's texts, and every one of them can, with a little straining of the reader's eyes, be found in the works of Mr. Bradley.

(a) "Do not," says Professor James, "condemn reality as soon as you find difficulty in seeing how it works. Be modest, and doubt whether you have seen rightly." This

[1] *A Pluralistic Universe*, p. 369.

is a gentle statement of Mr Bradley's judgment, which is,
"Your seeing is that of a sloppy-minded imbecile." They
join in condemning our poor attempts at interpretation.
"Dried specimens"; "bits cut with scissors," says Professor
James; "an unearthly ballet of bloodless categories[1]"; "a
spectral woof of impalpable abstractions," says Mr Bradley.
True it is that we must be modest; the falsehood lies in
denying that we have reached any reality at all.

(b) Professor James says: "Get full data." "The only
way in which to apprehend reality's thickness is either to
experience it directly by being a part of reality oneself, or
to evoke it in imagination by sympathetically divining
some one else's inner life[2]." "If you are to make out
the tunes rightly, you must open your ears to the whole
volume of sound." True, and most valuable. The falsehood only comes when he tries to maintain that the data
are the solution; that to see the stream is to see its make,
and to hear the noise is to hear the tunes. In being
myself I get my own experience in full, but how closely it
is often folded, how undiscovered are its treasures, how
little of its thickness do I apprehend! How seldom, in
short, can I see the go of it and of me. Mr Bradley's
share in this truth is obvious. His share in the falsehood
is, I think, more seeming than real, but those accuse him
of it who object to his "it must be and can be, therefore
it is." This, they say rightly, but I believe irrelevantly, is
no sufficient answer to "how is it?"

(c) "Here, then, inside of the minimal pulses of experience, is realised that very inner complexity which the
transcendentalist says only the absolute can genuinely

[1] *Logic*, p. 533.
[2] *A Pluralistic Universe*, pp. 250, 251. *The Hibbert Journal*, p. 571.

possess[1]." This is exactly what Mr Bradley says about feeling[2], and the truth and the danger are the same in both. Only Professor James seems to me to make the mistake which Mr Bradley is only accused of making; a failure to distinguish sufficiently between the folded and the unfolded unity.

Professor James returns to feeling in petulance, Mr Bradley in despondency. "These matters are too high for us," the latter writer seems to say now and then. "All our guesses are wrong; we cannot see how things are; let us cling to our knowledge that they are. Truth beyond this seems unattainable." This has usually been put down to Mr Bradley's agnosticism. Would it be unjust to take the other position as a result of too violent pragmatism? "We make truth. We make it very badly and with difficulty. Let us give up making it."

I have tried to write from the standpoint of those who conceive that reality does not wait for our thinking to make it, but that the discovery of reality does; that some discoveries can be made; and that it is the duty of philosophers to go on trying to make them. And in spite of everything this is presumably the real standpoint of all of us.

---

[1] *A Pluralistic Universe*, p. 284.
[2] *Appearance and Reality*, pp. 520—522.

CHAPTER VIII

ILLUSTRATIVE AND ADDITIONAL: THE APPRE-
HENSION OF FEELING

LET us conclude the first part of this essay with a chapter somewhat out of the main line of thought, and repeating in a different and independent way various arguments and dogmas which have been touched on before. A digression of this sort may perhaps serve to illustrate the concrete application of the method hitherto used, and to show certain consequences which appear to follow from the theory of knowledge which I have tried to set forth. This chapter will therefore consist of a self-contained essay on one of the current problems of philosophy—that of the possibility of apprehending our own feeling.

This is not the place for propounding or establishing a complete psychology of feeling, and I must therefore only explain quite briefly what my opinion of its nature is. We have used in this essay from the beginning the twofold and not the threefold division of mental process, treating conation-experience and feeling-experience as if they were related to each other far more closely than either of them to presentation. The doctrine I have assumed is practically the same as that set forth by Lipps in his latest edition of *Fühlen, Wollen, und Denken*. That is, I have assumed that the complement to presentative experience is the experience of activity, of striving. All feeling is activity-feeling, but toned in many ways— toned pleasantly or unpleasantly for instance. The matter of names is not important, and it might be preferable in some ways to describe the fundamental experience as conative, reserving the title of feeling for what Lipps calls the colouring or tone-quality[1]. But in the present chapter I shall generally use feeling as a short expression for the whole subjective side of our life.

A. *The Knowledge of Present Feeling.*

On the subject of our knowledge of present feeling I have little to say, and nothing new; and I am sorry to admit that the little which I have brings me once more into disagreement, or apparent disagreement, with Dr Stout. This great psychologist believes, as I cannot believe, that feeling which is present is *ipso facto* known. For him, it will be remembered, sensational experience, though cognitive, is not the apprehension of any object; hence, being provided with at least one example of a cognition which is not apprehension, he is not impeded by the ordinary difficulties in the way of a psychologist who has to claim a knowledge of present activity in a sense that would make a cognition apprehend itself as its own object. Dr Stout quotes Professor Ward as saying that you might as well suppose a man to put himself in a basket and carry himself. But his own point of view enables him to

[1] This, I think, would make the doctrine consistent with Dr Stout's. See his article in *The British Journal of Psychology*, Vol. II. See on the same subject Urban's *Valuation*, pp. 85—95.

avoid this difficulty. " I should say that a cognition knows itself against its object by a reflective process." " It seems to be an all-pervading fact of ordinary experience that the knowing consciousness is, however indistinctly, aware of itself. In being aware of an object we are aware of it as something known, and *eo ipso* we are aware of the correlative knowing....When we desire anything, we are aware of it as desired; it has a qualification which is absent in the case of an object which we do not desire.[1] "

My difficulty here is in the first place of course that on general grounds I believe knowledge to consist in apprehension, and that therefore Dr Ward's difficulty lies directly in my way and is insuperable. In the second place, it is that in the appeal to ordinary experience I cannot find enough to make me alter my general view. It is said that we know our desire, but it seems to me that such knowing is a reflective act, and that the primary process is simply to know-and-desire, to desire the known. Similarly in cognition, so far as I can see, we cognise what we apprehend, but not, in that same act, the act of apprehending itself. I would suggest that there may be a certain danger (of course not for Dr Stout himself) in the ambiguity of the phrase " conscious process." When this name is applied to a bodily event it implies that the event is known, that it is presented in sensation; but when it is applied to a mental event "conscious" seems to be the mere equivalent of "mental." That is, we use " conscious process" indifferently to mean " process of consciousness " and " process presented in consciousness," and we must not argue from one meaning to the other.

[1] *Arist. Soc.* 1905–6, p. 371.

I hold then that present feeling is not in the ordinary meaning known. Nevertheless I consider that in another sense it can be partly known, even while it still exists. What this knowledge is will become clear in the course of the examination of the second part of our subject, the apprehension of past feeling.

B. *The Knowledge of Past Feeling.*

If we take a first general glance at the subject the arguments which strike us seem to be two.

(*a*) At first sight we are, I think, inclined to say that we can remember our feelings. I remember a day at school when I was extremely happy, and I certainly seem to remember the happiness. "Do you not," it may be said, "perhaps remember the cause, and the attendant cognitions, and so infer, not remember, that you were happy?" The cause was and is entirely unknown to me; the mood came unexplained. The attendant circumstances were London streets, a fresh wind, and grey roofs shining in grey light after rain. There were organic sensations, I suppose, but I cannot say that I remember them. The happiness certainly seems at first sight not to be inferred but to be directly remembered.

Against this argument that we can remember feelings two different objections have been brought. One is, " This is not a remembrance, a presentation of feeling ; it is a revival. You put yourself in the old position, and are again glad." The other is, " You do not remember the happiness ; you only remember that you were happy." Both of these must be returned to later on.

(*β*) The second argument which occurs to us is a logical

deduction from the fact of our present investigation. "Here are we examining, judging, and investigating feeling. How can it be said that we do not know it ? If we judge, we must at least apprehend. Again, we can desire feelings and expect them, and be pleased or vexed with ourselves for having them. In all these cases is not feeling the object of our apprehension ? "

The objection brought against this argument is, "This is not knowing, but knowing about. You do not apprehend your feelings, but only that you did or will feel."

This answer evidently has the same sort of purport as the former statement that "we do not remember happiness, but only remember that we were happy." It is certainly very difficult sometimes to know what exactly we mean when we say that we remember. It will be wisest then to examine in the next place a few of the different things that remembering may mean. Or rather, not to tie ourselves to words, we will examine what we can do with a past process.

i. The simplest thing to do with a past process is to repeat it. I can submit myself again to a sensation ; can go again through the arguments for my beliefs ; can repeat to myself the poem which I learnt. We certainly use the word "remember" with this meaning sometimes. We say not only, "Do you remember that poem?" meaning "Can you repeat it"; but, in the same sense, "*Can* you remember it ? " This of course is the simplest thing to do with feeling. I can easily be happy again at the renewed thought of a piece of good fortune ; can revive my anger at an old injury. It is possible that sometimes when we speak of remembering feeling we mean only this. "Feeling-memory" in the sense of habit of feeling comes under this account. A cat of my acquaintance, having once caught his leg in a watch-chain and swung by it in the air, swore softly with a true revival of feeling whenever he met the watch-chain afterwards.

ii. Next, there is another thing we can do with a past process. We can, without really repeating it, play at repeating it. When I cannot look at the blue sky, I may image it. Instead of playing on the violin the tune I played just now, I may go over it in my head. When I have ceased to believe in the premises of my old faith, I may still go over the arguments that followed. Without *reviving* my belief, I may still *recall* it. Where I no longer know, I may still assume. I may project myself back into the old place[1].

One of the most interesting chapters in recent psychology is that which works out the similar process on the side of feeling. As I recall my sight of past snows, my belief in a lost leader, so can I recall the feelings which accompanied them, and in all these cases to recall is not to revive. As I can act through to myself a scene of youth in which I heard that I had failed in an examination, so can I call up the dull misery of the hour —can feel it in play as I hear the announcement in play. Since I know that this failure, by affecting my plans, really laid the foundation of future success, I am far from

[1] Cf. Professor Alexander in *Proc. Aristotelian Soc.* 1908–9. "Suppose ...I am remembering an event as happening to myself....The past object is before my mind, but it is not present. But my past self is present. It is an extension backwards of myself....We find just what we should expect to find if we understood mental events to be mere directions of consciousness. A past direction is a present consciousness."

being miserable about it now. In the same way I can share every sorrow of a hero of tragedy in the course of a uniformly pleasant evening.

This, I think, is very often what we mean when we speak of remembering feelings; and the failure to recognise the existence of these fancy-feelings has been the source of many of our difficulties of theory. For most people this way of remembering is easy enough—easier probably than imaging past organic sensations. We have only been induced to believe that we cannot recall feeling because we have disbelieved *a priori* in a recall distinct from revival. Whenever we succeeded in the easy task of play-feeling we have thought that we must be having the real feelings again[1].

Now, have we here a case of apprehending past feeling? When I first met with this chapter of psychology I thought we had. Now I am fairly sure that we have not.

German descriptions are obscure on this point by reason of their use of the same word, *Vorstellung,* for image and for presentation. Höfler[2], taking his account of fancy-feelings from an article of Witasek's, makes no

---

[1] Cf. Professor Alexander, *Proc. Aristotelian Soc.* 1908–9, pp. 35, 36. "Before it can be established that we have emotional or feeling memory we must show that we are not merely remembering the bodily accompaniments, or the attendant circumstances, or the provoking object, of a past emotion, and so reviving that emotion....We feel our present self extending backwards to the remembered event, and the pleasurable tinge in this experience is the ideal pleasure. It is quite distinguishable from the pleasure that we feel in the same object when actually present....It is a pleasure ideally present, referred to the past of myself, which past is called up by the memory of the external conditions under which it occurred."

[2] *Psychologie*, pp. 209, 210.

distinction between this sense of having feelings *vorgestellt* and the sense in which the psychologist has processes
vorgestellt when he examines them as objects. Witasek[1]
himself seems to take the fancy-feelings as presented.
But Meinong[2], still referring to Witasek, takes them as
analogous on the feeling side to assumptions on the
knowledge side, and therefore as being still of the nature
of feeling, and *not* objects of knowledge. In Meinong's
account, that is, they are not presentations but true
feeling-images.

I have little doubt myself that Meinong's treatment
is right. The *Scheingefühle* are still feelings, though not
"actual" feelings, not feelings-in-earnest, just as assumptions are still cognitive though they are not real beliefs.
We are not here apprehending our past feelings. We are
only playing at feeling them over again.

So far as we have gone, Dr Ward's objection to all
presentation of feeling still holds[3]. It is true that what
is not originally presentation cannot be made presentation
by being repeated, in earnest or in play. The question
is, then, whether we can do anything with a past process
except do it again. Is there such a thing as contemplation apart from, or over and above, repetition? We
shall find that our attempt to answer this question involves
the answer to the second of the two objections from which
we started, in that it obliges us to think out the connection between knowing and knowing-about.

[1] *Z. f. Psych.*, 1901. *Zur psychologischen Analyse der ästhetischen
Einfühlung.* In his more recent work on aesthetics Witasek takes fancy-
feelings to be ordinary feelings based on assumptions instead of on
judgments.

[2] *Ueber Annahmen.*

[3] *Ency. Brit.*, first article on *Psychology*, p. 44 b.

iii. Suppose that I see, on the dress of a saint in a stained glass window, a border of a peculiar shade of rose. I can, first, repeat this seeing by going to the church again. Secondly, without going to the church, I may visualise the tint. Thirdly, I may do more. I may remark to myself on the unusual nature of the colour. I may reflect that it occurred only in one other window of the church's magnificent series of ancient glass, and that I do not remember having seen it in any other church. I may wonder what particular process was used to produce it; may judge it to be a shade or two paler than a La France rose; may notice its rare harmony with the other colours in the window, and think it gives a tenderness and unexpected delicacy to the whole picture which could not be otherwise attained. In all these judgments I am apprehending that piece of colour which is their subject; and in all of them I am doing something more than merely repeat the process in which I apprehended it before.

Suppose that I have been taught in childhood a certain account of the history of this saint. I may go over it now in undisturbed faith. Or, if faith has disappeared, I may still go over the story as a story, without altering a detail. Thirdly, I may compare it with the histories of other saints, Christian and heathen. I may judge it to be beautiful, to be useful in education, to be fit to be taught as a parable if not as literal truth. I may form theories as to the way in which it arose. In all these thoughts I am apprehending in a new way the story which I used to believe and may still assume. This new apprehension is neither belief in the story nor assumption of it; but it is real apprehension nevertheless.

Finally, take my childhood's feelings towards this saint. If my faith has been retained I may revive them now, or something near them ; or by self-suggestion, even if my faith has been shaken, I may manage to repeat them. If I prefer it, I may without any illusion still play at taking the old place, still feel my old devotion in image though not in actuality. Thirdly, I may use contemplation other than repetition. I may estimate the value of these feelings in moral and religious develop-ment. I may note the history of their growth and decline, the way in which surroundings and interests helped them or hindered. I may see what they rested on ; remember the commonness of such feelings in the young. In all these judgments I apprehend their subject. In knowing these things I know feeling. This is the true apprehen-sion of past feeling. But further commentary is needed.

In examining this whole question of the know-ledge of feeling I was troubled by the apparent self-contradictoriness of the statement, "Feeling cannot be apprehended." How, I asked, could one make a judg-ment without apprehending its subject ? How could one think about a thing without thinking of it ? The last section has shown that I still maintain this objection. But I think now that the original statement, if carefully expressed, may be maintained as well. To examine this, let us as before leave the controversial ground of feeling and deal first with objects cognised.

(a) Take first my tint of rose-colour[1]. I can apprehend

---

[1] It will be just the same if I take, e.g. a movement sensation, which in popular language "only exists at the moment of sensing." I have not

it in image and sensation. I can also apprehend it in thought, as produced in the fifteenth century, as similar to the La France roses outside, yet not like them destined to fade; as connected with certain ether-vibrations; as a glory to the church. All this is real apprehension. I know the tint, not know about it. Yet it remains true that a blind man could be taught all this knowledge and still lack that knowledge which I had by sense. Or, to take an example which is much better because it is less likely to lead to irrelevant paths, if I were not able to visualise colour I could still have in absence all this apprehension of thought, could know in absence all the colour's history and its gloriousness. But the rose-ness of it I could get only by going to the church again.

Sense and thought, that is, know the same object, but what sense sees in it thought cannot see. Green was wrong in holding that perfectly adequate conception needs no sensation to fill it up[1]. Thought knows the object [I insist upon this] but not in its sensational capacity. If the eye of sense is considered as occupying the blind spot in the eye of thought, then we may say picturesquely that thought, in knowing our object, *knows about* that element in it which sense knows. Of course it is most important to remember the other side; that sense is blind to what thought sees, which is by far the greater part of what is in the object. But that does not affect us just here.

(*b*) So far the facts are clear enough. They are rather harder to see and fix when we come to the next level.

taken trouble to use examples of this sort, because their peculiarity seems to make no difference to my line of argument.

[1] *Works*, II. 190.

Take a statement in that history of the saint which I formerly believed. I can repeat my belief in it, or I can play at repeating and assume it. Thirdly, in contemplation other than repeating, I can apprehend its connections, history, value and the rest. This is still apprehension; it is acquaintance, immediate knowledge. I am said to be thinking about the statement, but really I am *thinking it about*. I am pulling it about, making it exhibit itself, putting it in new fields of thought to govern them, making it grow.

I am still apprehending the statement. But so far as I am not repeating my original apprehension, so far I am not apprehending just that in it which I apprehended before. The exhibition in new fields is new. I still know the object, but it-in-its-original-aspect I know-about.

With regard to both my instances, the colour in the glass and the history of the saint, what I am most afraid of is that emphasis may be laid on the second part of the last sentence to the overlooking of the first. I insist with all possible earnestness that if I know about I *know*. If I cannot visualise the appearance of the rose-coloured border, I can still know its position and value and uncommonness, its purpose and its history. I know that its tint is like that of a rose, different from a hyacinth, deeper than the sunset; unexpected, beautiful. My knowledge is not about it but of it. I know nearly all that is in it, that makes it; I know *it*. A man with the window in front of him, but with a concussion of the brain confining him to bare perceiving, would know the border too, but know less of it, less in it. Each of us knows it, and each knows-about that in it which the other knows. We must absolutely reject the plan of giving the titles of knowledge and acquaintance to sense-knowledge alone, and denying it to any apprehension in which only the sense-element is invisible.

It may be said that this is only a matter of words, that if we abstract and limit further, and take "the content of my sensation" for our "object," we shall have to say simply that thought knows about it without knowing it. No, for in this very judgment the "sense-content" has become an object of thought. And a thousand other judgments press in; the sense-content has a history, a place and date in my mental life, and relations to other contents; we can form theories as to its success in revealing the object; theories as to its difference from the sense-content of a colour-blind person looking at the window. The "object" of sense has indeed blossomed and swelled beyond the bounds of sense. No slip of reality can be cut so fine that it will not grow in the thought-field. No object can be made so microscopically small that it will not govern an infinite range of thought.

The difficulty lies indeed in explaining what it is that thought is debarred from. Did I say that the rose-ness was invisible to it? In that very judgment the rose-ness is apprehended. Fortunately explanation is helped by the fact that nearly everyone admits that there is a debarring, and knows the sort of exhibition which the object, rose-colour, gives in sense alone. I need only lay full emphasis on the other side, insisting that rose-colour is *known* not only in sense but in thought.

That which sense sees in an object thought cannot see; but it is a mistake to explain this as the result of a character of uniqueness or peculiar immediacy possessed by sense. It is simply a special case of the obvious rule that "so far as I am not repeating my original apprehension, so far I am not apprehending just that aspect of the object which I apprehended before." The exhibition in new fields must be new. If I ask a different question the object must give a different answer. Take a level where sense does not enter at all, and let our object be "the bishop who re-modelled Exeter Cathedral, completing the change from the Norman to the Decorated style." This is my first introduction to Bishop Grandisson, but I may deepen and enlarge my acquaintance with him afterwards. So far as I do not repeat my first apprehension of him, so far I do not know him in the original way. It is possible that I may cease to be able to recall that first knowledge. Yet I shall hardly be said to have ceased to know Grandisson because I am obliged to ask "What was it exactly that he had to do with the Cathedral?" Or it may be that my first introduction was to "a bishop of Exeter called Grandisson." Returning after some years, I may say "I know all about the bishop who re-modelled the Cathedral, but I cannot remember for the moment who he was"—meaning only "I have forgotten his name." It will scarcely be denied here that the so-called knowing-about is a better knowing than the original apprehension, but the original is omitted. Once more, let our object be the content of the assertion "St Dorothy sent flowers from heaven to the youth who loved her." This exhibition of the object is no more the end of it than the guide-book or passport description is the end of a man. I may think it about; may estimate the place of this incident in the story, its bearing on what precedes and follows, its value for the mediaeval or modern story-teller and poet, or for the child who hears it in a

Catholic school; I may think of its probable origin and
its possible use as an allegory. In all this I apprehend the
incident, but not just as I apprehended it to begin with.

The case of feeling is now probably clear enough.
I can apprehend it, and I do so whenever I make a judgment about it. But, as with sensation and belief, my
apprehension does not give me just that element, or aspect,
or exhibition of it which I had before. So far as I do not
repeat a process, so far I do not get just what that process
gave. Everything—everything in the widest and vaguest
sense—is a law-complex which works inexhaustibly, and
works differently in every field. Thought cannot exhaust
what enters in sense, but neither can sense exhaust it:
and feeling cannot exhaust feeling. My conclusion is,
then, that feeling and activity-consciousness are in just
the same position with regard to after-apprehension as are
the presented elements in consciousness. For each we may
use either repetition, or play-repetition, or apprehension-
other-than-repetition. So far as we do not repeat, so far we
do not get the same exhibition of the thing as we got before.

The sense in which I suggested that we might know
present feeling will now be clear also. We know it
when, and only when, our present act is to *think of our
present feeling*. In that sense I know it while I write
this passage. But in an ordinary act of cognition we
cannot know present feeling any more than we can see our
own face: it is not invisible, but we happen always to be
looking the other way. As in a ghost story, I leave my
past selves all along the road, and when I like I can turn
and see them. Nevertheless I cannot see what they saw,
nor can I feel what their attitudes felt like, except by

getting into them again. This is a perfectly possible proceeding, but it is a revival or recall of past process and not an apprehension of it. Between repetition and apprehension I have to choose.

Note. Our relation to the feelings of others will obviously come under the preceding account. I may share them in genuine sympathy: or I may play at sharing them, in imaginative *Einfühlung*: or I may apprehend them in that in thought I perceive what they are. That is, they may supply me both with primary or imaged feelings, and with objective contents of knowledge.

The investigation contained in this chapter was occasioned by the study of Professor Alexander's most suggestive and provocative paper on "Mental Activity in Willing and in Ideas[1]." I have come to agree with a good deal of its doctrine, but with one passage I am bound to disagree even more completely than I did at first reading of it. It appears on page 27 of the paper: "To me, I myself cannot be a *cognitum*, I can only be a *cognitum* to a being who stood outside both me and physical things, in the same way as I myself stand outside physical things and life. Life is an individual thing to the liver. But I can contemplate another being's life though I cannot live it. Now it is as impossible for me to contemplate my own mind as for an animal to live another animal's life. There is no reason, however, in the nature of things why a race of beings should not arise or be now in existence who can contemplate minds. Such beings would be of a higher order of mind and for them minds would be objects of knowledge."

[1] *Arist. Soc.* 1908–9.

I hope it is clear from the foregoing pages what my comment on this would be.

(1) I can and do contemplate my own mind as I contemplate physical things, and life, and anything else in the universe. Professor Alexander proves it by writing papers about his mind.

(2) But to contemplate is not the same as to live through. My contemplation of an animal's life is a qualitatively different experience from the animal's, and my contemplation of my own life is a different experience from the living of it; hence I can only contemplate the part which I am not engaged in living.

(3) As for the higher race of beings, they will have the advantage of being able to contemplate any part of my life they choose, since they are not engaged in living any of it; and they will presumably have the disadvantage of a much more limited access to what they want to know. So far they are in the same position as my next-door neighbour. If they are able by some means to share my feelings and thoughts, they may overcome the limit of access by living my life as well as contemplating it. They will then be in the same position as myself. Of course if they are cleverer than myself they will be able to do much more with that position. And if they can " enter into " my beliefs and feelings without being actually possessed by them, as I do fitfully with my past self and with other people, they will keep a calm and detachment of mind which will enable them to understand me much better than I understand myself. But I cannot imagine any other way than this. They can contemplate heaven and earth and myself and themselves, and so can I. And for all of us "seeing life" is a different thing from living it.

PART II

ERROR

CHAPTER IX

IS ANY KNOWLEDGE INFALLIBLE?

HITHERTO we have dealt with the nature of knowledge in the narrower sense of that term, without complicating the matter by consideration of the fact that cognition includes not only true knowledge but mistakes. We must now take account of this, and in order to guard against false accounts it will be necessary to begin by asking whether any part of cognition is free from this mixture. Is there any department of experience in which it is impossible to make a mistake?

No one, I believe, has ever claimed infallibility for inference, therefore we may confine our examination to uninferred knowledge. With regard to this we shall not even now attempt a complete enumeration of its different kinds, but shall only examine the most prominent. There are not many kinds for which infallibility has been seriously claimed.

1. The apprehension of *a priori* truths, such as the law of connection between premises and conclusion in a syllogism, is an instance of knowledge that is highly certain and trustworthy. The propositions apprehended are self-evident in a marked degree, and they are continually being

tested and easily justified by means of all our other knowledge and by new experiments. Since they are the basis
of inference, they cannot themselves be strictly inferred,
but they are plain without inference. Nevertheless this
self-evidence is clearly a matter of degree and not of
uniqueness of kind, for it varies with the simplicity of the
truth and not with its uninferrable nature. The connection between premises and conclusion in a first-figure
syllogism is no more *a priori* than the corresponding
connection in the fourth figure, yet it is undeniably easier
to see. In the second case indeed it is quite possible to
make a mistake. We must grant, then, that the cognition
of propositions of this kind is not as such infallible;
it is only on a high level of certainty because in the
most important cases the propositions are very easy to
apprehend.

2. Memory, which we have seen reason to class as uninferred, is undeniably fallible. Occasionally we attempt
to defend it by a shift of names;—when a recollection is
proved false we say of it not "I remembered" but "I
thought I remembered." But it has never been maintained that we have here a real difference in the quality
of our experience. A false memory is just the same sort
of experience as a true one; therefore memory as such is
not infallible.

3. Infallibility has sometimes been claimed for introspective judgments, but the claim has not often been made
by psychologists, who are too well aware of the difficulty
of introspection. In simple cases, certainly, introspective
knowledge is amongst the most certain that we have; it
is hardly possible to be mistaken in judging that I have
at this moment a visual sensation of marks on a white

ground and certain sensations of noise and of contact, nor
in judging that I am trying to write about the theory of
knowledge. But the judgments must be simple if they
are to be certain, hence introspection as such is not infallible. The belief that it is so has sometimes been made
more plausible by a confusion with two other things. One
is the certainty of that non-introspective, non-apprehen-
sive, "immediate" knowledge of our present feelings and
conations in which some writers believe. As was explained in the chapter on the apprehension of feeling, I
cannot see my way to believing that such knowledge exists
at all ; it appears to me that we feel our feelings, but that,
except in fallible reflection, we do not know them. The
other confusion is with the undeniable infallibility of
"simple apprehension" so far as it goes. This will be
explained presently.

4. The really serious question comes up in connection
with sensations. The opinion that these cannot go wrong
is of course a natural one for those who hold that sensations are "immediately given" in a way in which other
knowledge is not given ; but we have opposed this opinion,
urging on the one hand that all knowledge was "given,"
and on the other hand that the contents of sensation like
all other contents were presented as objects. What we
have to investigate is the claim of a special sort of given
contents to be necessarily true representatives of the
objects to which they belong.

The *prima facie* argument against this claim is the
existence of inappropriate sensations and of hallucinations.
A green rose-leaf is presented to a colour-blind man, and
it seems to him the same colour as the rose. A cold-spot
is stimulated by a warmed steel point, and we feel the

point as cold. A hypnotist suggests to his subject that the gold coin in his hand is burning him, and immediately the subject feels the burn. In all these cases have we not false sensations ?   The answer is instructive and valid. We have, it is said, nothing wrong here in the actual sensational experience. The error enters only in the perceptive judgment by which the sense-content is enlarged. There would have been no error had I judged that with my defective eye the tint of the rose is indistinguishable from that of the rose-leaf, or that the pain was a vivid image not connected with my hand. These true cognitions could still have contained the same sense-content as the false ones, as is shown by the fact that when my opinion is corrected the sense-content does often really remain unchanged ;—when I know that the steel point is warm I still feel it as cold. Sense-content, then, is independent of these errors and untouched both by them and by their correction. Therefore sense-experience is infallible.

Now the interesting point is that this kind of defence need not be confined to sense experience. Take an object of higher order such as we find in an illusion of direction or of comparative length. When we thoroughly understand the illusion-picture and know that the lines are really straight and parallel they may still appear markedly curved and convergent, and we say that there is no fault so long as we are not misled by the appearance. Or take a false memory. I remember an event in my childhood which I know from circumstantial evidence cannot possibly have occurred, and I find that this knowledge has not the least effect upon the clearness and firmness of the memory. I say naturally that I am not in error from this event appearing to me when I look towards my past, so long as I do not believe that it really did happen in my past. In common language we say that there can be no error in apprehending any object whatever, so long as I do not believe in it.

Belief, in this sense, is the apprehension of a content as belonging to a particular part of reality. There is no error in the sting of heat unless I connect it with the object touching me instead of my body, or with my body instead of my imaging mind. There is no error in remembering until I assign the scene to the actual past. I may think of the doings of wizards without the least error until I say " Wizards exist and in fact behave thus." The infallible way and the only way of avoiding error is to stop short of the line round our content at which it unites with a special and determinate universe of reality[1].

Thus it appears that the infallibility of sense is nothing but a special case of the infallibility of all such simple apprehension. Sense cannot lie, for it is incapable of pronouncing on the critical point ; in it we are too low for any distinction of universe. It is infallible not because of its immediacy but because of its inarticulateness.

The Search for Foundations of Knowledge.

It appears, then, that no knowledge worth speaking of is infallible. We must now represent that this makes very little difference to our security. The search for some infallible experience has nearly always been prompted by

[1] It is most important to remember that the *introspective judgment* "that I am apprehending this and that " is quite different from simple apprehension.

the desire to find safe foundations for our knowledge to rest on; but, as a matter of fact, on no foundation which has ever been proposed would our knowledge have had room to rest. Suppose that sense-knowledge in some concrete meaning of the term, or that introspective judgment, were to be proved infallible, and that on these we attempted to base the rest of our knowledge, how could it be done? The case would be different if every kind of uninferred knowledge were as such unerring, but for memory at least such unerringness has never been claimed, and yet we cannot proceed one step without trusting to memory. Nowhere in cognition is an unshakable foundation to be found for the mass and breadth of our belief.

The world of knowledge, in fact, is here in just the same position as the world of will. We find on the surface of the latter a mass and tangle of miscellaneous desires. Some of our purposes hang together and support one another, but some do not. Some are the embodiments of dispositions that lie deep in our nature and send their roots into every part of it; others seem to have scarcely any roots at all. Yet in all of them we are desiring, seeking, valuing. By their means we have to find out that way of life which is our good on the whole. In this good some of our present stray desires will certainly not be fulfilled, and we cannot find any department of desire which is safe from error of this sort. No one concrete purpose or valuation can be pronounced *a priori* to be certainly right, not even our most primitive instincts, or our most delicate intuitions, or our most faithful loyalty to general rules. Any one of these may, under certain circumstances, mislead us. Not one desire is infallible, and yet on the whole man does work out his good.

Knowledge without Foundations.

Are we then left, in ethics or in epistemology, with a castle in the air? The answer is neither new nor original.

We have found that "primary reality" in both worlds —the immediately given in every sense of immediate— the actually desired and actually cognised—provides in no department a safe and infallible foundation for the rest[1]. Everywhere, as experiences which primarily are indistinguishable, we have both right and wrong, both truth and mistake. A right desire or a true belief is not in itself a different sort of experience from the wrong and false; its self-evidence is the same; it is only by other evidence that we distinguish the two. Of no kind of experience can we say, Here error is impossible.

To defend the reality of the known universe by disputing this seems a plan exactly parallel to the defence of morals by intuitionist ethics. Since the beginning of morality there have been those who sought within value-experience for some infallible bit of experience on which the whole of conduct might be based. Some had intuitions of the Ten Commandments; some turned to our most elementary feelings and maintained that the perfect clue for our guidance lay there. Nevertheless the reply has always been made that in the first place not one of these valuations was unerring, and that in the second place, even if they had been unerring, each was too narrow and small to

[1] On the mixed nature of "primary reality" see a very interesting review of Mr Schiller by Dr Stout, in *Mind* for 1907. On this particular point I agree with Mr Schiller as against his critic.

provide the foundation of ethics. There is not one infallible desire, and yet the world of values stands firm, and
there is one kind of life and no other which is satisfactory
to man. Ethics has to be based not on any one part of
value-experience but on the whole character of humanity,
which can only reveal itself gradually, on a large scale, and
in many different ways.

So must it be with knowledge. No one particular
judgment of ours need be infallible, yet the universe
stands firm. In arithmetic, for instance, every one of our
operations is exposed to error, and yet the laws of number
hold and we find them out; and through our uncertain
operations we obtain an immense body of beautifully
established knowledge. So with the whole of cognition,
justified by the whole *Wirklichkeitszusammenhang*[1]. The
lack of unshakable foundations within experience is no
great matter, for every such foundation has turned out to
be far too narrow for the breadth of the structure. It is
enough that the world which manifests itself in the whole
of experience should be real.

[1] Lipps, *Bewusstsein und Gegenstände*, p. 98.

CHAPTER X

ERROR AND THE REAL

" IT is enough," we said at the end of the last chapter, "that the world which manifests itself in the whole of experience should be real." In the mixed contents of feeling and will a real world of character shows itself; in the mixed contents of cognition a real universe is presented. Now here we must go into more detail. What real object can be said to be presented in an erroneous apprehension?

In our original distinction between content and object we said that the object was progressively revealed in the content as investigation proceeded. This would seem to leave us in this case with a choice of descriptions. We may take the "object" in error either as that which we finally believe in, or as that which we believe in whilst the error still prevails. Either description will bring out some truth. The one looks on erroneous contents as being peculiar exhibitions of ordinary objects; the other takes them to be presentations of objects which in themselves are peculiar. We will begin with the first.

1. *Error as Abnormal Presentation.*

In this account we start from the fact that all mistakes
are imperfect apprehensions of the ordinary world. Something must be present with us in order even to be misunderstood. A column of figures, for one child in the
class, adds up to an amount not reached by any other
child or by the teacher. A man bearing pain heroically
appears to us as a man insensible to pain. A fictitious
injury, brooded over by a sullen-tempered person, appears
to him presently as an actual injury. In all these experiences, at the time when and in so far as the error is
true error, our attitude is that of the ordinary recipient
apprehension; if our mistake is genuine, we are not
choosing to make a mistake, but are receiving what comes
to us. What comes is a peculiar manifestation of the
object, because, presumably, there is something peculiar
in our conditioning body or mind. Nevertheless it is a
real manifestation of an ordinary object. One of the laws
that make up the very nature of $6 + 3$ is this: that for a
boy in a particular degree of hurry, with a particular
share of carelessness, it will add up to 10.

2. *Error as Presentation of Abnormal Objects.*

In the second description, instead of saying that the
peculiarities of our mind or body condition the particular
appearance of the " external " universe, we reckon them
along with this as elements in that given world which
appears. We have then no reason to say that any mode
of presentation is peculiar or abnormal, but instead we

comment on the peculiarity of some of the objects with which our life presents us.

In the first place, all these objects *are* presented, are actually seen. They are present with us, forced upon us, given and apprehended, just as certainly as any others. An erroneous content, like any other content, falls wholly on the object side of life. It is not an expression of myself in the sense in which an impulse or a feeling is an expression of myself; it is something given, to which I respond. To put it shortly, as before, when I am genuinely mistaken I am never *choosing* to make a mistake[1].

This means that all these objects in some way and to some extent are real, for they are proving themselves real—making themselves count. Nevertheless they are unable to count for much. Their self-evidence is there, but other evidence collapses about them. They break their promises; they rouse expectations and disappoint them; they contradict themselves. Presently we "see through them"; they become "transparent" fallacies. And finally they fade altogether out of our world.

Every object which can appear to us has reality enough to appear; it is for us to discover how much more reality it has. An ordinary object can appear on its own account, and it can do more, for it can appear to other people, and can keep its promises, and can affect other objects, and can often live with a life of its own. The object in error appears only parasitically, clinging to other objects, and in all the further tests it fails.

---

[1] If we say in the ordinary phrase that objects appear "to" the mind, then by the very force of words these objects, like all others, are "extra-mental."

No more than other objects is it created by our apprehension of it, but it has no more reality than serves it
to appear[1].

Other Accounts of Error.

Mistakes have been described in many other ways,
but we are cut off from using many of the descriptions
by the doctrines laid down in earlier parts of this essay.
We are not at liberty, for instance, to say in the usual
sense that error lies in the failure of our ideas to correspond with reality, and that truth lies in their success;
for in treating of true cognition we denied the existence
of any "ideas" between us and the real object. The
most we can say is that error means the failure of the
real world to appear to us in a normal way. Again, we
cannot express ourselves by saying that in error we construct wrongly, or combine the given wrongly; for we
have urged that knowledge is not construction or combination but apprehension only, and that not only elements
but the forms of their combination are presented to us.
Professor Alexander says[2] that a centaur consists of a real
head and a real body, and that I have only put the head
on the wrong body. But, in the first place, I did not put
it there; I had no choice in the matter, unless the case is
one of invention and not of error at all. And in the
second place the combination form is so essential a part
of the content presented that I remove only a very small

---

[1] This has to be carefully stated, for even in an erroneous object investigation may go on disclosing features without limit. Thin and
unstable as these objects are their *esse* is far more than *percipi*.

[2] *Aristotelian Society*, 1909–10.

part of error by asserting that the elements are not erroneous[1].

Nor, further, can we say that error consists in taking up a wrong attitude towards a real object—the attitude of belief instead of doubt or assumption; for we have laid it down that belief is characterised not by attitude or act but by content apprehended. Nor, I fear, can we adopt a very attractive account which makes error consist only in leaving things out, in failing to see all that is in the real object. In the way of its use there stands the objection that we do not attribute error where the content of knowledge is merely defective; we attribute it only when the content has an addition which is positively wrong. Where we believe a slander, for instance, our error lies not merely in our failure to perceive the alleged event as a work of imagination but in our apprehension of it as an actual event in a given person's life. Error is something more than ignorance.

Error Described, not Explained.

Our own accounts of the subject, even more than those we have avoided, are obviously not explanations but descriptions. The explanation of the possibility of making mistakes is far beyond the scope of this essay, and would involve the whole metaphysics of the relation of substance to its appearances and of the relation of mind to the universe. Our business here is only to guard ourselves

---

[1] The assertion itself seems highly doubtful. If I remember a tune wrongly at all what guarantee is there that it will not appear with a note which, as it happens, has never occurred in the actual world?

For excellent criticism of the combination view, see Dr Stout's article on " Error " in *Personal Idealism*, pp. 34-35.

against descriptions which seem misleading, and in particular to guard against any that would tend to weaken our hold of the fundamental axiom—that in true knowledge of whatever sort we have reality, in the fullest sense of that word, present in the mind.

Even a description of error, with explanation unattempted, forms indeed a crucial task for epistemology. The undeniable fact is that sometimes we know truly and sometimes we make mistakes; and in this we find a double-edged sword which threatens the two classes of theory. If in cognition we are in direct contact with real object how can we ever have error? If we are not, how can we ever have truth? To the present writer[1] it appears imperative to take the first alternative; and that means that all the chief difficulties in our way will be connected with this section of the essay. The writer is only too well aware of her incapacity for dealing with them in any way thorough enough to be satisfactory. The description may, however, be carried a little further, and may be so used as to make the difficulties themselves a little more vivid, which is perhaps the most desirable thing at present with a view to advancing the metaphysics of the subject. We may be able to obtain this vividness by means of a rigidly literal use of a certain ambiguity of ordinary language.

The Double Sense of Mind.

We hold fast even in the department of Error to the doctrine which we have professed from the beginning, namely that in so far as the mind is cognitive it is

---

[1] As also, I am very glad to observe, to Dr Stout. See his essay in *Personal Idealism.*

recipient only. To cognise is to apprehend the given. The object comes to the knower, comes before him ; and cannot be created or even affected by his recipience of it.

Yet in Error, apparently, something in the concrete event is affected, or even created, by peculiarities of the individual. An ordinary object appears to him in a way in which it does not appear to other persons, or to this person at other times ; or (taking our second account) an extraordinary object appears to him, which finds no place in the common course of nature.

The question is how both these statements can be true. How can the individual mind, receiving what is presented to it, be a factor in determining what object or what appearance of an object it shall receive ? It is the business of metaphysics to explain the possibility ; our business here is only to state consistently and in contrast the facts to be explained. This task would seem to be most conveniently performed by a frank use of the double meaning which popular usage attaches to our most important term.

We are accustomed in fact to speak of objects with equal readiness as presented " to " the mind and as presented " in " the mind. These uses are obviously incompatible, and involve a double meaning of " mind" which we may turn to our own account. Mind in the first sense must be that which apprehends the object; mind in the second sense is a factor in determining the appearance of the object. When a mind in the second sense is abnormal, the world must misrepresent itself to mind in the first sense.

I, it appears, sit within my mind, and any peculiarity in the atmosphere of that mind may affect the appearance of the objects which come before me. Or, I receive the objects mixed with my mind. The development of a presentation will reveal to me something of the world's character and something also of my mind's stupidity and fatigue. Or, in a vivid if difficult metaphor, the outer mind is the violin and the world is the bow, and I, the inner mind, am the hearer of the music. If the violin is defective the music will be spoilt[1].

With this description and distinction the subject must be left. The metaphysical questions which so evidently are raised must be answered in some other place than this essay.

---

[1] The metaphor is derived from Witasek's *Psychologie*, where it is used for a different purpose.

PART III

THE MANY-MANSIONED
UNIVERSE

CHAPTER XI

THE VARIOUSNESS OF REALITY

"Everything that is anything is an object[1]." The category of object, says Twardowski[2], is the most general possible; it is the *Ens* of Aristotle and the scholastics; it includes everything existent and non-existent. Every kind of cognition is the apprehension of some object. "Every presentation and every belief must have an object other than itself and, except in certain cases where mental existents happen to be concerned, extra-mental;...and ...the object of a thought, even when this object does not exist, has a being which is in no way dependent upon its being an object of thought[3]."

So far as I can see, in agreeing with this doctrine I am assuming no more than the simplest psychological account of cognition. I cannot apprehend without apprehending something. Cognition consists in the presentation of something in consciousness. The something is not my experiencing, for it is experienced. If it were

---

[1] Mally, in *Gegenstandstheorie und Psychologie*, p. 126.
[2] *Inhalt und Gegenstand*, p. 39.
[3] Russell, "Meinong's Theory," *Mind*, 1904, p. 204.

created at the moment I saw it and annihilated the moment I ceased to see it, it would still have a being not dependent on my act of seeing, since it would have been there for me to see. It is not an act of mine; it is not myself at all; it is the world in which I live.

It is simply a psychological fact that I actually have objects; that a world, of a nature to be continually determined, does come up against me, does enter my consciousness. Sensation and perception are names for coming across objects, apprehending them, in sense; an idea is the presentation of an object in thought. To say that I only know my own ideas can mean no more than that I do not know the objects which I do not know. The objects come to me and come against me, I reckon on them and must reckon with them, and therefore in that sense they are so far real. Some are to be reckoned with far more than others; and therefore have greater reality; they have more power of expansion, involve more, will show themselves in more lights and answer more questions. There is more to be made of a live man than of a man in a dream, especially after I have awakened from the dream. But, since they determine my seeing, since they are stuff that I apprehend, some reality is in them all.

At present all this seems to me so plain that it is difficult to argue about it. I seem to myself to be stating nothing but the barest facts of living[1]. Descartes only expressed half the basal certainty; for, since I think, not only must there be an I to think but there must be

---

[1] Russell says the theses in question are " generally rejected." Surely this implies some misunderstanding on his part, or on mine, or on the part of the major part of the world.

something that I think of. What I am, and what the something is, of course remains to be determined. But so far as this description goes realism appears to be unanswerable, and subjective idealism to be a most elaborate, unnecessary and ill-founded structure built upon it.

Let us then assume the truth of this form of realism, and go on to develop some of its consequences.

Universes of Reality.

It is clear that these different objects will fall conveniently into various groups. This is a fact of observation; it is by no means essential to the theory of realism. If all things had the same sort of reality, if no two had, if we never met the same object twice or if we never met any object but one, still if we met anything, if we were conscious at all, we should be apprehending a real world. As a matter of fact, however, we do find these different groups, and we speak of them conveniently as belonging to different universes of reality.

One great group, peculiarly interesting for all our practical purposes, is that of physical objects; existing in ordinary time and space. Closely connected with it yet not exactly identical with it is the world of "homeless" yet somehow actual objects; of notes and colours, of shapes and relations and complexes, of such "objectives" as hold good of the actual world. There is the world of the objects with which mathematics deals, and so on.

Besides these, there are groups more remote. The objects I meet in a dream are real, for they do meet me; but they are out of connection with the objects of my waking life. When I try to remember a dream, as opposed to trying to continue it, I have lost touch with these objects, and can only turn the former content into an object after the fashion of ordinary psychological investigation. But while the dream lasts I am exploring the object itself; asking continually not "What am I thinking of you?" but "What will you do next?" And the object proves its reality by doing. Then there are all the worlds of fiction. "The golden mountain of fairy-tale is as little identical with my image of it as the real mountain is identical with my image of it[1]." "Selbst wenn wir die Centauren oder die goldenen Berge des Märchens vorstellen, so sind sie für uns doch da draussen im Fabelland und nicht 'in uns'[2]." "When I judge that Athene was the daughter of Zeus, I am not making this statement about an idea in the heads of the Greeks[3]."

In contemplating these objects we are not making objects of our own processes. It is possible, however, to do this, and such objects will not fall behind others in their possession of trans-subjective reality. The objects of "inner perception," says Lipps, though they have not existence independent of my whole consciousness, are still independent of my present consciousness. "When once an experience has occurred it is a fact eternally real, whether or not I am now conscious of it[4]."

Finally, we must mention in particular a class which involves some special difficulties—that of objects with an internal inconsistency. We seem to meet with them when

<hr />

[1] A. Hoernle, *Mind*, 1907, p. 87.

[2] Munsterberg, *Psychologie*, p. 49.

[3] Meinong, *Stellung der Gegenstandstheorie*, p. 48.

[4] *Bewusstsein und Gegenstände*, p. 51.

for argument's sake we invent such a term as "green crimson," or whenever for practical purposes we employ a *reductio ad absurdum* proof[1]. I believe that these are real objects like the rest, but their reality has been denied and will need special examination presently.

Specification of Universe.

In ordinary judgment we seldom trouble to express in words the situation of the particular sphere of reality in which our objects exist. Sometimes this is only because the whole content of our thought is not put into words. If I describe an imaginary episode in a few sentences both I and my hearer are probably aware throughout that my statements refer to a non-actual universe, and it would be absurd to make an explicit assertion of this fact. Often, however, the nature of the universe concerned is not included in the content of cognition, though it is ready to appear there at any moment. When I read a novel for half an hour at a time I "know" that its universe is outside the actual world—that is to say that I should admit it at once if the question were raised; nevertheless throughout most of my reading the matter is not before my mind at all. I know it; there is no illusion; but I am not knowing it. I am interested in the universe of the novel, not in its relation to any other universe; and therefore I find it uncomfortable, and the focus of the picture is clumsily disturbed, if the author suddenly introduces a statement about a certain episode being founded or not founded on fact. But it is absolutely unfair to conclude that therefore my enjoyment of fiction is founded on

---

[1] Meinong, *Stellung der Gegenstandstheorie*, Chapter II.

illusion[1]. There is never illusion unless there is a mistake, and it seems very hard to be accused of making a mistake in a judgment of relation simply because I am not at the moment thinking about the relation at all.

Baldwin's account of our assignments of objects to their universes forms one of the best parts in *Thought and Things*. " Every object of cognition has subsistence[2] as simply made-up or present-existence comes later, when the object is determined as existing in one or other of alternate spheres. Existence is not a content added. It is rather an intent, an aspect of a content already made-up, whereby it is recognised as fulfilling a certain sort of expectation or demand made upon it." " An existential judgment often for the first time determines the real reference or control of a content which has already had formulation in a predicative or relational context. The relational meaning may be determined in the logical mode, while the real reference is still schematic, alternative, or quite undetermined. For example, I may say ' Sea-serpents hiss ' before I am at all prepared to say whether they exist or not, and in what realm." " Instead of saying with Bradley that in judging 'the sea-serpent exists' we have qualified the real world by the adjective of the sea-serpent, I should say that we have qualified the sea-serpent by the adjective of realness of a restricted sort. The 'realness' is constituted just by the...recognition of the sea-serpent as a ' controlled ' content. Of course, after

[1] As e.g. Hoernle, *Mind*, 1907, p. 88.

[2] Baldwin says that his " subsistence " is equivalent to Meinong's *Bestand*; but in Meinong's usage we deny *Bestand* of e.g. relations which do not hold (such as the difference between two exactly similar things). For Baldwin these have subsistence since they are objects of thought. More words are needed.

reality as a logical universal has arisen, we may use it substantively to the various contents as adjectives, as is seen especially in negative judgments of existence." "The pre-supposition of a sphere of existence or reality is always the sleeping-partner in the entire firm-meaning expressed as 'Content, Ltd.' until this partner claims the right, in the existential judgment, to have his name written out in the firm-title, ' Content, Reality, & Co.[1] '"

Notes on Difference of Universe.

Confusion occurs when the task of remembering the distinction between two universes becomes too delicate and difficult for us. Sometimes, however, we seem to fall into the other mistake of forgetting identity. To a schoolboy, and indeed I think to most of us, the personages of a remote period of history fail to appear as in a world continuous with our own. They are not actual to us; we think of the time-series of their lives almost as if it were the time-series of a novel; not as part of the time in which we live. I do not know whether it shows a peculiar defect in my intelligence that I find the same difficulty even with people and events of the present day if they belong to distant parts of the world.

Of course, since " universe of reality " is no more than a picturesque name for kind or department of reality, it will often be indifferent whether we speak of two universes or of divisions of one universe, or of one universe qualified in a certain way, or thought of in abstraction from some property which really belongs to it. It depends on our

[1] *Thought and Things*, Vol. i., pp. 240, 241; Vol. ii., pp. 20, 21, 25.

own taste whether we say that the older writers on
political economy dealt with our actual world or with
some other.   And when a remark is prefaced by the
phrase "humanly speaking" I am never sure, nor do I
think the speaker is always sure, whether it is meant to
apply to actual fact or not.   But we must be prepared to
recognise divisions when they are convenient, unless we
are to put too great a strain on our psychology.   Such a
strain appears to be involved in all attempts to impose
the same centre or scheme of localisation on all universes.
When I say "I have just been enjoying the scent of these
roses," the reality apprehended is naturally and suitably
described as being "continuous with present perception."
But the description is very much less appropriate when we
say "The death of her first child was a terrible shock to my
sister," and it becomes almost absurd when our judgments
are "Pharaoh's daughter walked by the river," "Perdita
was abandoned on the sea-coast of Bohemia," and "Of
imaginary curves of such a kind the following equation
holds." The reality of these objects is no doubt continuous
with that of present perception in the sense that by taking
pains we could find the way round.   But this way round
does not enter into our ordinary thought.   Nor, even when
we do see something of it, need that element which is
nearest actuality be also nearest the centre of the picture.
In a historical novel we usually date the real events
with reference to the fictitious events, and not these by
those.

As we must allow each universe the right to its own
schemes of localisation, so must we allow to each its own
sense of "existential judgment," and its own distinction
between necessary truths and truths of mere fact.   We

may have a merely categorical judgment within a fictitious as well as within the actual world. Contrast " The
Utopians are a singularly orderly nation " with " If another
nation attacked them they would naturally defend themselves in the following way." The distinction between
categorical and conditional would be no clearer if these
judgments referred to the inhabitants of Germany[1].

[1] This in criticism of the mode of expression in Bosanquet's *Logic*,
Vol. I., pp. 116, 215.

CHAPTER XII

ASSUMPTIONS

AMONGST the objects just described occur some which have a peculiar and interesting quality, in that they are created by our own choice. At the moment of apprehension I deliberately determine the character of the object I am to apprehend. I can do this in the actual world, by building three ships and seeing them completed. Or I can do it in non-actual worlds by means simply of the fiat, "Let there be three ships." That is, I can *assume.*

Assumption in its ordinary concrete use is a double-sided term, and we must be careful not to confuse the two elements it implies. We create our objects, and in the same moment we apprehend them, and the two processes are as distinct as they are in the building and seeing of an actual ship. The being of an assumption-object is in no way dependent upon my apprehension of it, inevitable though that apprehension is. It is dependent upon the act of creation alone. The cognitive element in an assumption differs in no way from any other cognition. Here as elsewhere cognition is nothing but the presentation of reality in consciousness, only in this case the reality presented is our own creation.

The Peculiarity of Creation by Assumption.

When I write a chapter in a novel I do in a different universe precisely what I do when in the actual world I build a ship. I enlarge reality ; create more objects for the apprehension of myself and of others. These objects would be real if they were only presented once and then destroyed and forgotten; but in most cases they have much more reality than this, since they are capable of being presented again and again, of being looked at in various aspects, of being explored and developed in consciousness to an indefinite extent.

The only difficulty in this matter seems to lie in the distinction of universes. It is not always easy to keep one's mind clear as to the exact kind of reality which has been created.

To begin with, we have the ambiguity of the phrase " Let there be——," "Let it be so." The effect of this is sometimes an alteration in the actual world ; it is the fiat of creation in this world. More often, however, we intend to make no such alteration but only to assume it. The actual change does not occur in the world of actuality. Our assumption has *reference to* the actual world, but creates its object in the sphere of fiction.

Next, take a universe which is already non-actual. Let it be that of a novel in course of composition. " Henry is not yet utterly depraved. Let him be placed in a position of responsibility and it may save him yet. If a sudden and striking call were to come he could probably pull himself together. But no such chance of redemption is to be granted him." That is, even in the fictitious world of the novel, the events I apprehend are not to be actual. My assumption has reference to the novel universe, but creates its object in a world more fictitious still. I create against the background of the novel but in a different material[1].

Thus we may lay down the rule that assumption never creates in the universe to which it refers. A new universe is always introduced, one remove further from actuality. I can assume an assumption—"Suppose your opponent in this game of chess were to think of your attacking him thus." Or I may make the hero of my play write a novel in which the heroine writes a short story describing the writing of an epic. Every assumption brings in a new universe without the slightest confusion; every creation is in a new material.

Finally, as before, an object in each of these universes has its own sort of existence. A high golden mountain is not "actually" high, nor does an existent golden mountain actually exist, since they do not enter actuality at all. But in their own universe they are high and they do exist[2]. The word "actually" is indeed quite ambiguous on this account.

Conative Analogy for Assumption.

When Mr Hoernle, in a passage quoted above, suggested that our enjoyment of fiction rested on illusion, he supported his argument by the observation that a wish

---

[1] In such a phrase as "Let ABC be an equilateral triangle" there is the same ambiguity as we noticed at first. With regard to the universe of real space I am assuming; in the universe of fictitious geometrical figures I am creating. If I am concerned only with a piece of paper that lies before me, then my phrase expresses no assumption but a simple imperative issuing in a bodily action. It is in exactly the same case as "Let us build a ship." "Let us imagine a triangle" lies between the two. In regard to the world of images it is actual creation, in regard to that of sense-perception it may fairly be called assumption.

[2] Cf. Meinong, *Stellung der Gegenstandstheorie*, p. 17.

can only be maintained if we suppress the collision of its idea with reality, and that if it is maintained it tends to become a desire. I urge that this analogy is wrong. A wish belongs to my "actual" self; it is an incipient desire, kept from passing into action by the fact that the resistance of the environment (to neglect more complicated cases) makes action hopeless. This is analogous to an object which is apprehended in the actual world and which yet is unable, on account of the weakness of my mind, to gain my full attention and to work itself out in full and consistent belief. If my puzzle-headedness gave way a little my attention would be gained and the development would take place. If the mental weakness increased even the marginal apprehension would disappear. Similarly Mr Hoernle is right in saying that any relaxation of the known pressure of the environment will turn the wish into a desire (and then into an impulse), whilst an increase of the restraining pressure may abolish it even as a wish[1].

If then a wish in the conative sphere does not correspond to an assumption in the cognitive, what shall we say is the true conative analogy for assuming?

So far as I can see, the following is the proper line of argument. When we assume, conation enters in a peculiar way into the cognitive world. Normally it enters only in the activity of apprehending objects which were already real, as when we look round to acquire new perceptions, or as when we draw inferences from facts which we know.

[1] For the whole scheme of the cognitive-conative analogy as I see it I must refer to my *Logic of Will*. When I wrote this, however, I was unacquainted with the notion of *Scheingefühle*, and the scheme might now be greatly extended by their means.

But in assumption we have not only a new apprehension, but a new object is created for us to apprehend. So in the analogy cognition must enter peculiarly into the conative sphere. Its normal entrance develops our established dispositions by setting before us new objects which would satisfy established desires, or by finding means to our ends ; but in the case analogous to assumption it must so enter as to create a new disposition in us. Further, the new object which is created by assuming has a reality which is not that of the actual world, and therefore the new disposition must be separated from the actual in some equivalent way.

It appears to me that these conditions are satisfied by a slight modification of Meinong's answer to the problem. For him the analogy for assumption is a "Phantasiegefühl[1]." I should prefer to say that it was a fantasy-*desire*. "If I were the last person left alive in the world and my cat were the last animal, I should greatly desire that the cat should remain alive and fond of me." Here is a desire which is cut off from actuality as an ordinary wish is not cut off. The person supposed to be concerned need not even be myself; I have fantasy-desires when in watching a play or in reading a powerful novel I take upon myself the impulse and feeling of the hero of the drama.

In assumption and in dramatic desiring we have analogous creations, of objective and subjective elements which are not actual and which yet in their special way are real. In assumption the actual world has nothing added to it, except in the sense that an event of assumption has actually taken place. But the whole real universe is increased, because the newly created object has such

---

[1] See, e.g., *Über Annahmen*.

reality that at least one presentation of it is possible. In *Einfühlung* or in any fantasy-conation the complex of dispositions which makes my actual self has nothing added to it, except by means of this exercising and strengthening of my emotional imagination. But my whole self, which is not merely the actual, is increased, for I have added the personality of another to my own, with such reality as allows of at least some of his conations existing in me. By force of Shakespeare's invention the universe contains both himself and Othello. By force of the sympathy of a lad in his audience that lad's self contains not only himself but Othello as well[1].

Returning to Mr Hoernle's statements, we see that this change in analogy has freed assumption from its connection with illusion. The passage into actual desire and conation is normal for an actual wish but not for a fantasy-impulse. Similarly assumption in itself, apart from confusion and error, involves no blending of universes.

Truth and Falsehood in Assumption-Worlds.

There is no real Ivanhoe, says Professor James, but as many different Ivanhoes as there are different minds cognisant of the story. An alteration in one man's version does not affect that of any other man, and we are confusing universes if we appeal from our differences to the idea in Scott's mind[2]. One would say that common opinion would hardly go so far as Professor James. It is true

---

[1] Of course in this contrast of the actual with the rest of the real no disparagement of the former is intended. That which actually exists, which actually happens, which is actually true, has by far the fullest and richest kind of reality.

[2] *The Meaning of Truth*, pp. 27, 28.

that we change universes if we begin to speak of Scott
where we have hitherto spoken only of Wilfrid and
Rowena; whilst we are reading intelligently we are not
regarding these personages as ideas in the author's mind.
Nevertheless we should surely feel ourselves justified in
appealing, not to " Scott's idea," but to the " real " story,
related in this case in a particular book. If anyone departs
from this account of events we do not hesitate to say that
he has gone wrong; and for this very reason his alterations
fail to affect our own views. The case would be altered of
course if our companion declared his intention of writing
a new novel on the same subject as Scott; we should then
have to make it clear in future (not which author we meant
to imitate, but) to which version we meant to conform.

It is a curious but inevitable fact that the creator of
any world has the rights of a despot within it just so far
as he chooses to employ those rights. If Shakespeare
makes Sir Toby get drunk every day then he does get
drunk, and no regrets on the part of a reader can make
him respectable company for Olivia. Yet the impossibility
is partly determined by the very fact that the author has
not chosen to be an absolutely arbitrary despot. The
drunkenness he decreed, but for the rest he left his world
to be governed by the ordinary law of actuality, that
people who behave in this way are not respectable. In
general all created worlds conform to these laws except so
far as their creators explicitly abolish them. It is false
to say that princes are ever turned into swans, or that
a man can live when he is marble from the waist down,
or that the noise of breaking ice can become a man,
unless some German peasant or Arab or Esquimaux has
declared with authority that it shall be true.

It is surely far less paradoxical to extend our theory of truth and error so as to cover statements in these assumption-worlds than to follow Professor James[1] in refusing to extend them. These objects which we partly create and for which we partly borrow life from the ordinary world have life in them from both sides. They have solidity and resistance. Their presentation in consciousness can develop harmoniously in one way and not in another way. We can argue about any good novel; can maintain not only "Ivanhoe did this," but also "He would never have done that." Of course there are limits to the definiteness of structure which enables us thus to argue, because in no humanly created world can creation be so concrete as to determine everything. It is neither true nor false to say that Viola had brown hair. And a bad novel is harder to argue about than a good, because its personages have so much less in them.

Now there is another reason on account of which a bad novel may baffle our arguments. That is, it may have a definite structure which is inconsistent with itself. It is exceedingly difficult to discuss the probable colour of a heroine's hair if in Chapter 1 her eyes are a velvety brown and in Chapter 8 they are sapphire blue. So again we may be baffled by Dr Venn's bad theologian[2], who inquires what the duty of a Christian would be in case his God issued an immoral command. We cannot argue; not only because the given laws of our universe are not extensive enough, but because their nature invalidates the ordinary convention that in case of doubt we proceed on the laws of the actual world. Here we only

[1] And Mr Russell? See the next section.
[2] *Empirical Logic*, p. 390.

140 ASSUMPTIONS

know that one of the most fundamental of these laws, that of non-contradiction, does not hold ; and it is exceedingly difficult to say what is left to guide us. We know, moreover, that the inventor himself is not prepared to decide the question (as he has the right to do), because he has not noticed what he has done. If he did know it, it would be much better worth while to discuss the consequences, and we might be able to give him advice on the most reasonable method of procedure.

This brings us to a curious and interesting subject— that of objects which are deliberately created with an inconsistency in their natures.

The Problem of Self-Contradictory Objects.

What are we to say of such objects as "a pentagon with six corners," or "crimson green"?

They evidently create many difficulties, and the simplest plan would be to deny that there were any such objects. Yet in every presentation something must be presented. Therefore we must take one or other of two alternatives; we must either deny that any presentation at all corresponds to such phrases as those given above, or else we must hold that what is presented is not what at first sight it seems to be. These are the only methods by which we can avoid the admission of self-contradictory objects into some universe.

The first method is that used by Lipps[1]. The thought corresponding to such phrases, he says, is only an attempt at thought. It is not merely that we cannot image the objects, for we can and must think of many things which

[1] *Bewusstsein und Gegenstände*, pp. 60—62.

we are unable to image—infinite space for instance. It is that we cannot think of them at all. The second plan is Mr Russell's[1]. When we use the phrases in question objects are denoted, but objects of a singularly remote and complicated kind, which contain no inconsistency.

Lipps' solution seems to me to be blocked by psychological facts. The phrases which indicate self-contradictory objects are used intelligently; they are not mere complexes of sounds, and it seems impossible that no real thought should correspond to them. A *reductio ad absurdum* proof, gone through with a knowledge of what the end will be—gone through therefore as a deliberate examination of a self-contradictory object, is surely not a mere attempt at thought. Mr Russell's solution allows it to be considered as good and intelligent thought, and indeed at first sight he seems to attribute to us an almost unheard-of degree of intelligence. Introspection is difficult, and when the question is raised it is not always possible to tell exactly what we have been thinking of; yet I felt it at first impossible to believe that in an ordinary quiet moment of my life, when I did not know that I was doing anything extraordinary, I had really been contemplating the objects described by Mr Russell. On consideration, however, this would seem to be hardly a fair objection, for we may contemplate the most complicated object without noticing its complication provided that it only shows us part of itself, or that it is presented with a fallacious appearance of simplicity.

The real objection to both accounts is, to my mind, the limits they set to our imagination. When I set out deliberately to think of a self-contradictory object, can

[1] " On Denoting," *Mind*, 1905.

I not do so ?   No assumption-object, after all, has reality
unless I, by assuming it, deliberately give it reality.   In
all such bestowal of reality I depart from the strict law of
the actual world and create a world which is partly new.
Cannot I, if I so wish and purpose, set the law of non-
contradiction aside ?   Against Lipps I maintain that in
all the present discussion I am thinking, and am therefore
thinking of an object, and *ipso facto* of a real object.   As
against Mr Russell I maintain that the objects I think
of are by no means so difficult to apprehend as the things
which in his view my phrases denote, but that on the
contrary they are comparatively simple though self-
contradictory presentments.   I am glad to find myself
here in agreement with Professor Meinong.   Dr Stout
appears to disagree[1], yet he says that an object is real if
it is possible to make a mistake or even to conceive a
mistake concerning it[2]; and certainly in the matter of
self-contradictory objects Mr Russell conceives that
Professor Meinong is making a mistake.

Content and Object.

Not only is the object of my thought self-contradictory,
but that part or aspect of it which enters my thought
includes the self-contradiction.   Here as on the general
relation of content and object I differ from Twardowski,
who says that the content can never contain a self-
contradiction, and that therefore the object must be real

---

[1] *Personal Idealism*, article on "Error," p. 37.   "There is only one
conceivable way in which the abstract object can be unreal. It may be
unreal because by its own intrinsic nature it is incapable of existing. But
this can be the case only when it is internally incoherent."

[2] *Op. cit.* p. 38.

in order that it may do so. The content, he says, must exist, and therefore cannot be inconsistent; the object may be inconsistent, for it is real without existing[1]. In my view both can be inconsistent because neither of them exists. I myself am the only actual existent in the case, unless we apply the term to my act of apprehension, which actually occurs.

The Truth about Self-Contradictory Objects.

We now return to the problem we approached before. What is truth, in a universe where by hypothesis a self-contradiction does not involve falsehood ?

The difficulty seems to be no more than an unusually acute case of indeterminateness. In the universe of ordinary fiction, it is true to say that Sir Toby is a drunkard and neither true nor false to say that Viola has brown hair. It is false to say that Viola is capable of murdering Sebastian for money:—not because this incapability is ever asserted, but because the creator of this universe has evidently taken over from the actual universe the law that human beings cannot absolutely belie their characters. For similar reasons it is true to assert that while Orsino is in his own garden he cannot be in Olivia's. But we find greater difficulties in a universe where we know that one self-contradiction at least is according to law. Are we to consider the law of non-contradiction as abrogated altogether, or is it to hold except in this one case ? and how far does this exempted case extend ? The creator of the universe must decide, but if he has not

---

[1] *Inhalt und Gegenstand*, p. 23.

decided we must presume that he followed the ordinary conventions of world-making, and then we may fairly discuss what in this case the convention would naturally decree.

Meinong's decision seems to me a fair one. In my way of putting the matter, it amounts to saying that the ordinary laws must be supposed to hold wherever they are not explicitly denied. The same reason which makes it true to say that green grass is green and that a golden mountain is golden, also requires us to say that a round square is round[1]. The roundness of a square is an impossible *Sosein,* nevertheless the roundness of a round square is not impossible but necessary[2]. Similarly an existent round square is existent though of course it cannot actually exist[3].

As far as I understand the dispute, Mr Russell would have no special reason to object to this solution if he could admit that the self-contradictory objects were real at all. His fundamental difficulty lies only in their initial breach of the law of non-contradiction. Meinong urges that this

[1] *Gegenstandstheorie und Psychologie,* p. 8.

[2] Mally, *op. cit.,* pp. 128, 129.

[3] It is existent, that is, just as it is round, in its own universe. Russell seems to miss this point when he says that he can see no difference between "is existent" and "exists" (*Mind,* 1907, p. 439). The words of course are ambiguous and indifferent ; " to exist actually" only means "to be existent in the actual world." But the distinction of universes is all-important, and has nothing special to do with the self-contradiction in these objects. I create for myself at this moment the object of thought "an existent plane figure with 973 one-inch sides." This is existent in its own universe, for I have decreed it so, and its sides are of the required number and length. But it will not be existent in the actual world until I take the trouble to draw it. Shakespeare creates a house for Olivia, and it exists, but is not "actually" existent. Cf. *Stellung der Gegenstandstheorie,* pp. 16, 17.

law applies undamaged to all that is actual or possible[1], but Mr Russell objects that it is of propositions, not of subjects, that the law is asserted, and that " to suppose that two contradictory propositions can both be true seems equally inadmissible whatever their subjects may be[2]." I suppose Meinong would reply that it was not equally inadmissible; that the law applied to assertions made with reference to the actual world, not to the worlds which we made for ourselves.

The question perhaps reduces itself to a matter of words and of convenience in the end. It would be possible without inconsistency to limit the term "reality" to such objects as are either actual or connected with the actual world in a way in which fictitious objects are not connected. Sir Toby would still be a real object, but only as being an actual invention of Shakespeare's. It would be false to say that he was a drunkard. It would be true to say "Shakespeare says that Viola had a brother," but false to say either that she would or that she would not have murdered him. This is, I think, a consistent usage, but I do not consider it the most convenient. I am not quite sure whether or not it is Mr Russell's. To clear up that point, and to settle the question on its own merits, it would be well for the disputants to discuss it with regard to fiction as a whole, without complicating matters by seeming to confine themselves to the special and bizarre case of self-contradictory objects.

[1] *Stellung der Gegenstandstheorie*, pp. 16, 17.
[2] *Mind*, 1907, p. 439.

CHAPTER XIII

THE MUTUAL RELATIONS OF JUDGMENT, APPREHEN-
SION, ASSUMPTION AND DOUBT

ACCORDING to my view, the fundamental need in a treatment of knowledge is to recognise that every instance of knowledge is an instance of the presentation of reality in consciousness; or, regarded from the other side, an instance of the apprehension of reality. When this is once settled, the disposal of our various special terms is not much more than a question of convenience, and many uses may be equally justified so long as we make ourselves clear.

If we are to mark out judgment from the rest of apprehension, there are perhaps two or three chief ways open to us. We may say that we judge when we apprehend an object as belonging to the world of actuality or validity; as being non-fictitious. Or we may use the term whenever we assign an object to its special universe, whether or not that universe is the actual world. Personally I should prefer the second alternative. Our distinction would then be equivalent to that by which Professor Baldwin distinguishes belief; "The particular control which assigns a thought to a sphere of existence,

inner, external, semblant, or other[1]." Thirdly, we may
adopt a different distinction and say that to judge is to
apprehend an object of higher order. This would include
all the cases which fell under the other descriptions, for
existence in any sphere is an object of higher order.

I think that it matters very little which of these alternatives we adopt, but an important point comes next.
When we apprehend any of these objects we have no
choice, as we have several times remarked, as to what we
shall apprehend. We can decide whether or not we shall
see anything—whether we shall look that way. But once
we have looked we have no choice of what we shall see.
When we have asked a question there is but one answer.
We speak of assigning objects to this sphere or to that,
but neither objects nor contents wait for any directions
from us. Denying a proposition is a very different matter
from denying a request. When we deny the existence of
an object the cognitive part of the process consists of
nothing more than the apprehension that the object does
not exist. To believe in an object is to see the content
show forth the object's position in its universe, and not
in any sense to put it there or even to consent to its
being there.

Now since an act, in any sense in which it is relevant
for our distinctions, must be capable of being a choice, and
since in these matters we have no choice, we must keep to
the doctrine we have held throughout, that in all cognition
the act is of the same sort, consisting simply in apprehending; in opening our eyes on a particular level and looking
in a particular direction to see what is there. Judgment
is marked out from the lower and simpler kinds of appre-

[1] *Thought and Things*, Vol. ii., pp. 21—23.

hension by a peculiarity in the content apprehended, and by a *consequent* peculiarity in the act of sight, but in no other way.

I must therefore disagree entirely with the doctrine of some of Meinong's school, that "judgment and apprehension differ neither in object nor in content, but in act[1]." "The conviction that justice exists is different from the imaginative contemplation of a righteous world[2]." Yes, for the content of our apprehension is different; in the first case we see our justice living and growing in the actual course of events, in the second case we see it only in a non-actual universe; or perhaps we only see it incomplete, disjoined at the edges from any universe. Besides knowing the characteristics of justice, we know that it is doubtful whether or not it exists.

Meinong's own method is to distinguish judgment from mere presentation by two characteristics—the presence of belief, and determination "with regard to yes and no[3]." For my account, both these points belong to content and not to act. To believe is to see the connection between object and universe; and to affirm or deny, so far as it is cognition at all, is to apprehend the presence or absence of objects. This latter point is evident, I think, when we avoid the confusion pointed out by Mr Russell, between rejecting P and apprehending not-P[4]. The denial of a request comes under the first head; it is the opposite of consenting to that request, and differs from it primarily in act. The denial of a proposition is the opposite of affirming that proposition, and differs from it primarily in content.

[1] Witasek, *Psychologie*, p. 280.   [2] *Op. cit.*, p. 78.

[3] E.g. in *Über Annahmen*.

[4] *Mind*, 1904, p. 348. Or see p. 46 of the present essay.

Assumption and Judgment.

The foregoing decisions will evidently have some bearing on the position of assumption in the whole of knowledge.

We must remind ourselves to begin with that the term in question is the name of a concrete process which includes more than cognition. When we assume, we create an object as well as apprehend it. Hence it is certain that assumption in the concrete will differ "in act" from judgment and from the rest of apprehension, but the important question for us is only, "Does the cognitive element in an assumption differ thus in act from the rest of cognition?" My answer must evidently be once more that it differs in act only in so far as it differs in the content apprehended. In assumption my object is partly of my own creation, and I know it. I need not always have the fact in mind; I may be attending to internal details so intently that the object's relation to the actual world is not in consciousness at all. But unless confusion and mistake supervene I never see the object as actual; whereas in judgment this is what I do see. That means that there is a difference in what I have in mind, in the content and the whole object of consciousness.

"The revolution began yesterday" has its object in the actual universe; "Suppose that the revolution had begun yesterday" has it definitely not there. That is, though the limited part of our object expressed by the term "revolution" may be the same in assumption and in judgment, the whole object presented to us is not the same. Even the limited part, we may say, is made in the two cases of two different materials.

If the objects differ in this way, does it follow that it is impossible to find an assumption and a judgment whose object shall be the same ? The answer is determined by that peculiarity of assumption-creation which prevents the creation from ever taking place in the universe to which the assumption refers. If judgment by definition has to keep its object always in the actual universe it is impossible for an assumption-object to be identical with it, but if we allow the term to refer to other universes then the identity can be obtained by the device of making judgment and assumption refer not to the same but to neighbouring worlds. The best instances will be supplied by the writing and reading of historical novels. The author in the course of composition, referring to a historical personage, makes the assumption that "The Emperor expressed himself thus." This assumption refers to the actual world but makes its creation in the novel's world. The reader, thinking and judging in the latter, says, "The Emperor uttered the following words." Here we have an assumption and a judgment with the same content, and we observe that all the difference between them has disappeared.

The great writer who has been the first to see the importance for logic and psychology of the study of assumptions has given an account of them which differs in some fundamental points from mine. Judgment, according to him, differs from mere presentation in two characters both of which belong to the act, namely in that it involves belief and in that it affirms or denies. Assumptions keep the affirmation or denial but drop the belief[1]. They are

---

[1] *Über Annahmen*, p. 2.

much nearer to judgment than to presentation, for it is quite intelligible to speak of them as judgment without belief, but unintelligible to say that they are presentations determined with regard to yes or no[1].

Mere presentation (*Vorstellung*) makes the weak point to my mind in all parts of Meinong's philosophy. He himself is hindered by it; it does not fit in with his classifications, and is apt to make an exception to all his rules[2]. I suggest that the whole difficulty comes from attempting to distinguish the different forms of cognition as different acts instead of making them all apprehensions with various contents. For me the yes-no determination and the belief are both a matter of content. Mere presentation, if we wish, may be harmlessly defined as presentation lacking these characters. It is much more doubtful whether they can still be counted as two characters and not rather as one, for both seem to consist in the kind of connection which is seen to exist between our central content and the rest of reality. I have therefore worked throughout with a different definition, keeping closer to ordinary language, and have made the differentia of assumption consist in the fact that in it I deliberately create for contemplation a non-actual object. Then if belief is taken in Baldwin's sense to mean the sight of the object as having position in a special universe, not necessarily in the actual universe, we must grant that in assumption belief is still present as well as affirmation and negation. For we know in what way our assumption-object does and does not exist.

Witasek's development of Meinong's account shows the

---

[1] *Op. cit.*, pp. 277–8.
[2] See e.g. *Über Annahmen, passim.*

danger involved in describing assumptions as judgments-without-conviction. Assumptions, according to Witasek, are very closely related to judgments, for they lack nothing except belief, and the amount of belief that is present in a judgment may vary in amount to any extent[1].—True, a judgment that began with full conviction may lose that conviction bit by bit; the landscape that seemed solid and distinct may become more and more misty; what we saw clearly may fade away until it vanishes. But the end of this scale of doubt is anything but an assumption; the end is suspense of judgment, absence of cognition. "It is absolutely certain that the murder took place thus and here" may be weakened through "It is probable that it happened thus" and "We cannot be quite sure that it happened thus" into "It is quite uncertain whether there ever was a murder." But by no natural process of cognition does this become "I will write an account of the murder for the *Daily Mail*."

This may become rather more evident when we have examined the position of doubt as such.

Doubt, Judgment and Assumption.

Not only assumption and judgment but doubt and judgment differ in their content. In judgment the map is complete; the central object is seen in position within its universe. In doubt of the existential sort we see the central object but it is not clear to us whether it has a proper connection with the universe or not. The mountain stands out clearly but mist encircles it, so that we cannot be sure whether it is a real part of the landscape or only a mirage.

[1] *Psychologie*, p. 310.

Nevertheless the mountain may be real; that is, belief in it and doubt as to it may have the same object in spite of their difference in content. An assumed mountain on the other hand can never be thus real, nor, except by confusion, can it ever come to appear so. It is encircled by no line of mist; its edges stand out in the void against the background of that actual landscape of which it can never become a part. We have no doubt here; the object is non-actual and we know it.

It is therefore extremely important to keep clear of any confusion of assumption with doubt. Doubt may properly become belief as the mist clears away. Assumption never can. Even if we assume a hypothesis which turns out to be true, the belief is continuous not with our assumption but with our doubt. It occurs to us that the object half hidden in mist may have a certain shape;— here is the germ of belief. For the sake of experiment we sketch that shape; construct it to stand out on the mist. Having our eye thus guided, we are able to discern more and more clearly that this in truth is the shape of the mountain behind. But though the appearance of the mountain looms up and fills out our picture, the picture is no more than a vision and a help to the eye. When we have done with this it vanishes; it never becomes part of the mountain, for its material is not granite but empty air.

In constructive hypothesis I apprehend an object created by me, and thus enable myself to apprehend an object which I did not create; but in that second cognition I am not assuming. The real object appears to me, never in so far as I assume, but in so far as I begin to believe. Of course there may be all kinds of mixtures and confusions. An object long and vividly assumed may through self-suggestion come to be believed in, just as by the same process a fantasy-desire or fantasy-impulse may burst the bounds of its universe and blend with actual will. In a fit of melodramatic jealousy or resentment a man may experience all these possibilities. But in so far as our procedure is rational our will grows not from fantasy-desire but from actual craving, and our belief develops not out of assumption but out of " opining."

PART IV

CONCLUSION

CHAPTER XIV

THE PRESENTATION OF REALITY

"It may be," says Professor James, "that the truest of all beliefs shall be that in trans-subjective realities. It certainly seems the truest, for no rival belief is as voluminously satisfactory....Anticipating the result of the general truth-processes of mankind, I begin with the abstract notion of an objective reality. I postulate it...[1]."

I cannot decide whether I am bolder or more modest than Professor James in beginning with what I take to be not the postulate but the certainty, not the abstract notion but the concrete unavoidable presence, of an objectively real world. Is it that I attribute to our experience more than he feels justified in attributing to it, or is it that he demands more than I before he will call a thing objective and real?

All that I demand is that the object's being shall be independent of our apprehension in the sense that this act of apprehension has not created it. This condition is satisfied by every object that enters our consciousness, for apprehension can create nothing. If we had invented the

---

[1] *The Meaning of Truth*, p. 243.

universe as we might invent a novel, I should still call it objective and real. If every object were created at the moment when we observed it and annihilated the moment we ceased to observe it I should still use the same terms. Since we really have experience, it is in my usage inevitable that there should be a real world. Such reality has been defined as the limitation of activity[1], but it is also the tool and material and basis of activity ; it is support as well as resistance. "What we must take account of" is "what we can count on."

If there is any presentation there must be a real world. But now, this reality being granted, the world develops before us. Some of it we do invent, but for the most part it invents itself. Some of it never recurs, but some does. That is, it behaves twice in the same way, and therefore *ipso facto* it is in so far the same ; I have nothing to do with any numerical identity which is different from qualitative or working identity. Some of it is ready to recur whenever we choose ; two and three make five whenever we like to add them. Some of it appears with the same behaviour in all manner of different shapes, and thus we find the laws of causation, and the relations of space, and the operations of time. An immense and indefinite amount is added to what we have to reckon on and reckon with, in that we apprehend not only the behavings of the world but these ways of its behaviour.

Every presented object has such reality as enables it to present itself, but most objects have far more. Not only do they present themselves now and here, but if we take proper steps they will present themselves otherwise ; and not only do they present themselves to us but they

[1] Baldwin, quoting Stout.

affect one another—the evidence for this being that in sense and in inference we see them do so. Parts of the universe have most complex and interesting ways of behaviour, and these parts we call fellow-men. We know them as different from ordinary things partly by their resistance and incalculableness[1], but still more because they can help us and co-operate with us much better than a thing will do. They are known as human not only because they overthrow our expectations but because we can expect so much more of them. Complex as their customs are, they present themselves with a certain naturalness and intelligibility. We learn readily to understand and depend upon them. Indeed the process of early development consists scarcely so much in learning to expect a certain behaviour here as in learning not to expect it from the rest of the world. Our discoveries consist less in finding that some of the universe is personal than in finding that some of it is not personal.

Since our powers of apprehension are not confined to sense, therefore we apprehend in the personal part not only bodies but minds. In all cognition, and not only in perception or sensation, or uninferred knowledge, reality is in my sense directly presented. Hence we have direct apprehension of other men's natures and of other men's experience. We find that their experience of outer objects is to a very large extent the same as our own ; that is, our external world is for the most part qualitatively identical, and, as before, I have nothing to do with any non-qualitative identity. As a matter of history, our discoveries consist rather of finding that some of the universe is not common than of finding that some of it is ; for, owing to

[1] Baldwin.

the nature of our practical life, the commonness of important and interesting objects is forced on us as soon as we meet with the object at all. From the beginning our sensory experience, for instance, is supplemented by what in thought we perceive of other men's sensory experience. Further, we apprehend not only the experiences which other men share with us, but their private experience as well. Their feelings and thoughts are sometimes harder to perceive than the motions of their bodies, but often they are much easier. These also form part of the universe which we know.

Finally, in these matters as in all others mistakes are possible and often actual. Sometimes what has presented itself as bread reveals itself presently as a stone. Sometimes what has presented itself as a man reveals itself as a lifeless thing. It is abstractly conceivable, though not credible, that the loaves in our larder are all stones, that all the objects we have believed to be men are really lifeless machines, that England is not really an island, and that the integral calculus is founded on an immense mistake. If all this were found to be so the world would greatly change its shape for us. Nevertheless the world, the *real* world, would in some shape remain. Whilst we live we cannot escape from this intimate presence, this inevitable and undeniable pressure of objective reality. Whilst experience exists there is a real person and a real universe.

INDEX OF AUTHORS REFERRED TO

For EU product safety concerns, contact us at Calle de José Abascal, 56–1°,
28003 Madrid, Spain or eugpsr@cambridge.org.

·

www.ingramcontent.com/pod-product-compliance
Ingram Content Group UK Ltd.
Pitfield, Milton Keynes, MK11 3LW, UK
UKHW020315140625
459647UK00018B/1883